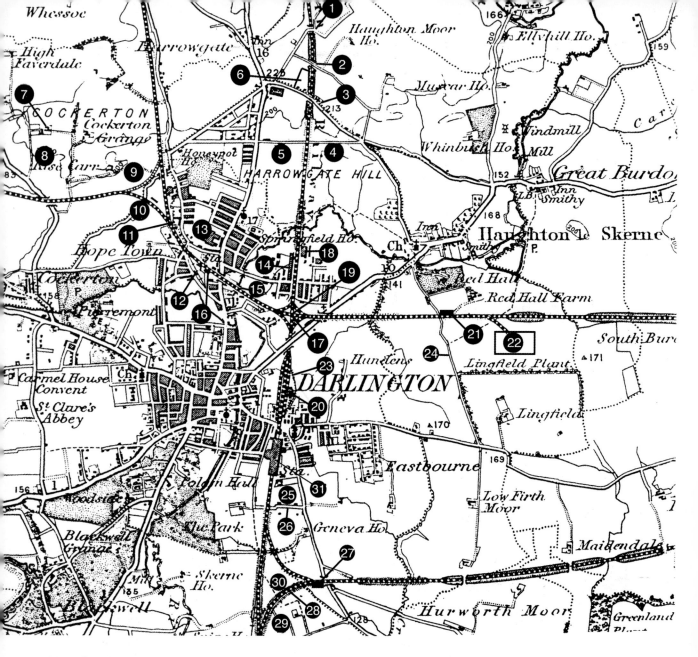

Map of Darlington indicating key locations.

1	Glebe Road	17	Great North of England Railway engine shed
2	Green Lane	18	Darlington Wiremills
3	Salters Lane North	19	S&D Crossing
4	Robert Stephenson's & Hawthorn Works	20	Bank Top shed
5	Thompson Street East	21	McMullen Road signal-box
6	Penrose's Market Garden	22	Paton and Baldwin's Factory
7	Faverdale Hall	23	Dead line
8	Faverdale Wagon Works	24	McMullen Road
9	Stooperdale Curve	25	Cleveland Bridge engineering works
10	Hopetown Curve	26	Smithfield Road
11	NER shed, Whessoe Crossing	27	Geneva signal-box
12	Scrapyard	28	Geneva Curve
13	North Road locomotive works	29	Snipe House Junction
14	Darlington Forge	30	Engineers' Reclamation Depot
15	Skerne Bridge	31	Bank Top station
16	North Road station		

The Last Days of Steam Around
DARLINGTON

Class K1 no. 62003 heading south with a brake van to pick up its train, probably at Croft yards, in spring 1962. A Northallerton engine at this time, it was transferred to Darlington on closure of the shed in February 1963.

The Last Days of Steam Around
DARLINGTON

DAVID BURDON

SUTTON PUBLISHING

First published in 2003 by
Sutton Publishing Limited · Phoenix Mill
Thrupp · Stroud · Gloucestershire · GL5 2BU

British Library Cataloguing in Publication Data
A catalogue record for this book is available from the British Library

ISBN 0-7509-3158-2

Endpapers: Class V2 no. 60895 leaves Bank Top station with a train of coal-wagons on 7 July 1964 as Class J94 hurries away to its next duty.

Half-title page photograph: A classy line-up at Top Bank in June 1962: Class A1 no. 60127 *Wilson Worsdell* standing alongside Class A4 no. 60006 *Sir Ralph Wedgwood* and Fairburn tank no. 42085.

Title page photograph: Darlington-based Class K1 no. 62001 in July 1964 heading north on the outskirts of town.

Typeset in 10/12 pt Palatino.
Typesetting and origination by
Sutton Publishing Limited.
Printed and bound in England by
J.H. Haynes & Co. Ltd, Sparkford.

Foreword

The opening of the Stockton & Darlington Railway on 27 September 1825 for the locomotive-hauled transportation of paying passengers as well as coal traffic symbolised the beginning of the steam railway era, and Darlington became recognised worldwide as the birthplace of the railways. Of course railways and wagon ways had been around for centuries in various forms.

Darlington rather than Stockton evolved into a principal railway manufacturing centre as it was advantageous both financially and geographically to the S&D system. North Road Locomotive works was opened on 1 January 1863 under S&D ownership but by the time the first new locomotive had been built in October 1864 the S&D and NER had amalgamated. In later years Stooperdale Boiler Shops (1911), Bank Top shed (1903, rebuilt 1938), Robert Stephenson's & Hawthorn Locomotive works (1901) and Faverdale Wagon works (1923), along with various supplier companies, all developed, making the railway industry Darlington's major employer, providing employment for over a century. All this collapsed with the contraction of the railway network and Beeching's modernisation plan. These factories ceased operations during 1963–6, throwing thousands of Darlingtonians out of work.

This book depicts steam workings around Darlington in the final years, mainly from 1960 to 1966. Even though steam was in rapid decline during this period it was, nonetheless, a very interesting time. North Road works stayed busy almost to the end as it took over steam repairs previously done by Doncaster, Derby and Horwich works, as well as continuing to maintain its traditional NER/LNER stock. In 1961–3 there was an influx of LMS 2-6-4 tank engines which worked the remaining branch line parcels traffic as well as carrying out shed and station duties. Darlington shed also had the responsibility of running-in ex-works engines and preparing them for return to their home sheds, and in 1964/5 dealt with ex-LMS and BR standard classes as well as ex-LNER Pacifics which had visited North Road works for repair. These would all previously have been overhauled at other works.

The first sign of the decline of steam operations at Bank Top shed (code 51A) came in the late 1950s with the displacement of the Class A5s, A8s and L1s from the passenger branch-line services to make way for diesel railcars. The introduction of the English Electric Type 4 main line diesels in 1958 had little noticeable impact on express steam workings at first, but as their numbers increased and reinforcements arrived in the shape of British Railways-built 'Peaks', English Electric Deltics and Brush Type 4 diesels the writing was on the wall for the Pacifics, although some of the lucky ones displaced to Scotland lasted into late 1966. The inter-yard transfer of freight, mainly coal, declined rapidly after 1963 as the south-west Durham collieries closed down, and scrapping of the steam shunters, mainly Class J94s, commenced. They had disappeared by July 1965. The main line steam standby Pacifics, nos 60124 *Kenilworth* and 60145 *St Mungo*, were present right until the end when the shed closed on 26 March 1966. These were the last of the LNER's final Pacific design. All were broken up, although a twenty-first-century version is under construction in the S&D carriage works at Hopetown, near the Railway Museum. The remaining K1s, WDs and Ivatt Class 4s were dispersed to other sheds. The furore over the closure of North Road Works had overshadowed Bank Top Shed's demise. This double blow in early 1966 severed Darlington's last links to the steam railway after more than 140 years.

Introduction

Icannot remember suddenly realising that I was interested in railways, but they were always part of my life. My father joined the LNER at Gateshead works in 1927 and transferred to Darlington North Road works in 1938. As a sheet-metal worker he was exempt from war service. I was born in 1941 and most of my childhood spare time was spent by the railway bridges at Salters Lane North or Thompson St East at the north end of Darlington near the Robert Stephenson's & Hawthorn works. New engines could be seen in the works yard, but most were for export and left by road. My uncle was a coppersmith at Heaton shed, Newcastle, and he took me there for my first-ever visit to a locomotive shed when I was about nine or ten. The cab ride on a Class V2 no. 60812 was my first.

My mother's family all lived at Keswick and we would go to visit them three or four times a year. We took the Stainmore line to Penrith, then changed to the Cockermouth, Keswick & Penrith Railway for the last 18 miles to Keswick. I can recall the train coming to a standstill on one of the great viaducts, either Deepdale or Tees, and we looked down from the open window on to the treetops way below. I travelled this route many times but regretfully took very few photographs. The Barnard Castle to Kirkby Stephen section would have been a massive attraction, had it survived.

When I was a bit older I was left in my aunt's care at Keswick for Easter and school summer holidays and from here I would catch a diesel railcar to Penrith and Carlisle making many unofficial visits to Upperby, Kingmoor and Canal sheds. From the seat on the opposite side to the driver you could see the oncoming trains and keep an eye on the speedometer. The DMU would clock over 70 mph on the long curve between Penruddock and Blencow. Summer Sunday excursions arrived at Keswick with Black Fives, Jubilees and even Royal Scots in charge. I spent many happy days at Penrith station where a bell would ring continuously to signal the approach of nonstopping expresses and through freights. Carlisle-bound trains would come off Shap Fell and thunder through the station on the tilted curve. The speed and noise was very impressive, even frightening when you were standing on the down platform when they went through.

These idyllic years came to an abrupt end in August 1957 when I began my working life as an apprentice fitter at the North Road Locomotive works. My father had some influence there, and got me an interview. After a cursory medical, arithmetic and English test, I was accepted. Part of the English test was to spell Edinburgh, Middlesbrough and Scarborough. My first job was on a shaping machine in the shell shop and after a couple of years moving around the various departments I was transferred to the main erecting shop to work on the reconstruction of steam and diesel engines.

By this time I had become part of a small group of apprentices who were interested in steam engines outside work. Unfortunately this interest had to be kept low-key or we would be subject to ridicule from the majority of non-like-minded workmates. Many hundreds of locomotives visited the works during my 5½ year apprenticeship. I never took my camera in during working hours, although I did so at weekends, often visiting my own place of work with RCTS parties.

Summer Sunday bus trips in 1961–3 to visit sheds in the Leeds, Manchester and Liverpool areas, saw a 6 a.m. start by Grierson's bus from under Darlington town clock. The first stop was usually Starbeck shed at Harrogate at about 7 a.m. Shed visits would

Class A1 no. 60151 *Midlothian* passing through Heighington station with a southbound express on a Sunday in September 1952. Heighington is situated on the former Stockton & Darlington Railway route between Darlington and Shildon. Trains were being diverted via Bishop Auckland as the engineers had possession of the East Coast Main Line. It was here that the steam age began in earnest after George Stephenson's *Locomotion No. 1* was transferred to the track after being hauled by road from his works in Newcastle on 16 September 1825. A practice run by *Locomotion No. 1* with a coachload of officials in tow went from Shildon to Darlington on 26 September 1825. On the next day the historic journey from Shildon to Stockton took place. This sparked off the events that led to Darlington's evolution into a major railway engineering centre. The Class A1, the pinnacle of steam development on the LNER, owes its existence to events here 127 years earlier. (*Geoff Jackson*)

continue all day until dusk or later if the shed foreman would let us in. We would often return home in the early hours of the following day.

I began taking photographs with a simple box camera in about 1960. It had only one shutter speed and an aperture marked 'bright' or 'dull'. Consequently, I could not take any pictures of moving engines. Even so I produced some decent shed shots. Many years later I decided to catalogue them and was surprised to list over 700. I invested in a Baldessa 35mm camera in 1962 and later bought a Pentax. Photography wasn't an exact science to me, shutter speed and aperture being set largely by guesswork, although experience produced reasonable results. I carried out my own developing and enlarging.

Shortly after completing my apprenticeship and leaving the works I was touring the Scottish sheds in the summer of 1963, by Lambretta scooter, when I was in a collision with a cattle wagon near Huntly and spent two weeks in Aberdeen hospital with a broken leg and other injuries. I used the four month's convalescence to lineside around Darlington. I bought my first car, an Austin Cambridge, with the compensation. I was free then to travel further afield, Carnforth, Shap, the Settle and Carlisle Railway and Carlisle being my favourite places.

I was married on 26 March 1966 – on the very day Bank Top shed closed. Not unnaturally, this produced a conflict of interests for me and in retrospect I didn't cover the last couple of years of steam operation as thoroughly as I could have. After the end of BR steam my prints and negatives lay unseen for thirty years. Then, owing to redundancy, I had some time on my hands and my interest in them was rekindled. I am no expert on the workings of steam locomotives, nor of coaching stock or the finer points of railway operations. I just loved watching steam trains in action and pointed my camera in the right direction more in hope than expectation.

In the last few years I have visited Wolsztyn in Poland and the Harz system in Germany, but three weeks in China watching and photographing real steam in action was a fantastic experience. Visits to large steam sheds and the Changchun locomotive works evoked many happy memories, although compared to North Road works it was shambolic and dangerous.

I hope you enjoy these photographs of steam working around Darlington in the 1960s. Thanks must go to Doug Hardy for allowing me to use some of his photographs. The late Geoff Jackson and I exchanged negatives many years ago, and I am certain that the inclusion of some of his work would have met with his approval. Thanks must also go to my wife Chris for her help in typing the text on the word processor. It would have been a long job for a one-fingered operator!

Opposite above: There's plenty of power here as Class WDs Nos 90081 and 90451 pause to raise steam at Bank Top shed in February 1963 ready to clear the local branches of snow. Snowfall may have been light at Darlington but places such as Richmond, Barnard Castle and Crook were on higher terrain and suffered accordingly in winter. Note the long fire-iron propped against the telegraph pole. This enabled the fireman to reach the far corners of the firebox on these 126-ton engines.

Opposite below: Class J27 no. 65882 ex-works at Bank Top shed, 25 June 1964. Just in front of it is Pacific Class A1 no. 60124 *Kenilworth*, also just out of North Road works. No. 65882 will return home to one of the Blyth sheds. It was built at Darlington for the NER in 1922 and withdrawn in September 1967.

Fowler Class 4 2–6–4T no. 42405 simmers at Bank Top shed on 5 May 1963. Of 1933 design and fitted with cab doors and side-windows, it arrived at 51A in October 1962 from Sowerby Bridge Shed (56E) to replace withdrawn ex-LMS locomotives nos 40190 and 42553. No. 42405 lasted until November 1964 when it was taken out of service.

These 0–6–0 saddle tanks were designed by Riddles for war work in 1943 and the LNER bought seventy-five in 1946 when the War Department had no further use for them. They handled most of the shunting and inter-yard work around Darlington, assisted by a few Class J72s. They were classed J94 by LNER and around fifteen were at Darlington in 1961–2 before scrapping began. Here no. 68050 takes a mixed freight from the Croft yards north behind Bank Top on 12 June 1963. The LMS tank engine behind it is no. 42085.

A shed check on 19 June 1965 showed 27 steam engines comprising 9 ex-LMR engines, 1 Pacific, 3 V2s, 1 B1, 9 K1s, 1 J27 and 3 WDs. There were no Class J94s. Nos 68010/47/53 were the last in service, being noted at 51A on 13 March 1965 with six others in store. Nos 68010/11/23/37/43/47/53/60/62, all from 51A, were sent to Cohen's scrapyard at Cargo Fleet, Middlesbrough, in August 1965.

Class J27 no. 65859 out of use at Bank Top shed, June 1964. The cooling towers and chimneys were Darlington's main landmark, visible from the A66 some 20 miles away on the Pennines near Bowes.

Darlington class B1 4–6–0 no. 61353 returns home under Green Lane bridge, 5 April 1963. All the over-bridges on the main line were being raised in preparation for electrification, which didn't actually happen for another thirty years. No. 61353 was built in Darlington in 1949 and sent to Rugby Testing Plant for experimental blast-pipe and chimney tests.

Class Q6 0–8–0 no. 63393 heads north with a train of steel ingots from Teesside on 20 July 1963, apparently preferring to go the long way round instead of taking the more direct Bowesfield Junction (Stockton) to Ferryhill route. The Q6s were classed as T2s by the NER. Darlington built thirty in 1913 then waited another four years before producing another twenty in 1917, ten in 1918 and ten in 1919.

The embankments were graced with a profusion of wild flowers as fires kept the undergrowth relatively short. Here Class A3 no. 60061 *Pretty Polly* approaches Ketton bridge with an Up passenger train in early June 1963. This Grantham-based engine had only three months left in service, as it was withdrawn in September 1963.

Class Q6 0–8–0 no. 63443 on the Simpasture branch approaching the Great North Road over-bridge at Aycliffe from the east. In the distance are the protection signals for Ricknall crossing. The signal-box is disused and stripped of all its equipment. The Q6s were the NER's main heavy freight engines. They were designed by Sir Vincent Raven and building began in 1913 at Darlington works, where 70 of the 120 class total were constructed. Armstrong-Whitworth Co. built the remaining 50, the last appearing in 1920.

Class V2 no. 60895 of York MPD heads north near the Stockton & Darlington crossing at Albert Hill in Darlington on a dark morning in October 1964. Behind is Llewellyn Wynn Williams Railway Engineers factory.

Class V2 no. 60974 at Darlington, 1 May 1963. The south end of platform no. 1 was the best place to be if you didn't want to miss anything (except when a DMU obstructed the view).

Ivatt CL 4MT no. 43129 takes a train of chaldron-type coal-hoppers north past Penrose's market garden with Salters Lane bridge in the distance, July 1964. This was a regular Bank Top working.

Class WD no. 90309 of Darlington shed, heading north with a load of flat steel sheets, is pictured here near Danby Wiske, in March 1963. Surprisingly, it was allowed through on the Down main line rather than on the slow line. The slow lines were removed when steam was phased out. No. 90309 was called into works for a general overhaul in November 1963.

Class J72 no. 69006 passes under Haughton Road bridge heading for Bank Top sidings, 17 July 1963. This engine was one of the batch built by British Railways at Darlington works in 1949, fifty years after the original design appeared. No. 69006 went for scrap in December 1963.

Class Q6 no. 63368 (still showing a 54D Consett shed-plate) undergoing repairs at Bank Top sheds with a Class WD 2–8–0 and a Darlington-based DMU. This shed-plate should have been changed to 52K when the shed groups were reorganised. The 54 group code was abolished.

Class Q6 no. 63398 takes coal east on the Stockton & Darlington Railway, 20 July 1963. The Redhall housing estate now occupies the land on the right. The spur on the left enters Paton & Baldwin's factory. The section of the Stockton & Darlington crossing to McMullen Road was closed on 21 May 1967. A single track was left from Oak Tree junction back to McMullen Road from the opposite direction to allow access to Arnott Young's scrapyard at Fighting Cocks and Paton & Baldwin's factory. The signal-box at Fighting Cocks was demolished, and the level crossing gates were operated by the train crew.

Class J39s in North Road works yard in March 1963. Sadly, their next move was to the scrapyard. The J39s were the most numerous class to come out of North Road works. Of the total 289 locomotives ordered by the LNER, Darlington built 261 between 1926 and 1941. Built for freight, their use on passenger turns was not uncommon as the 5ft 2in diameter wheels gave a fair turn of speed.

Class J21 no. 65110, still with a full tender of coal, has made its last journey to Darlington scrapyard in June 1960. Its last duties were at Heaton carriage sidings (Newcastle), where it was active as recently as April 1960.

Class WD 2–8–0 no. 90482 from Hull Dairycoates waits at Arnott and Young's sidings for its call into the scrapyard in May 1967. All its working parts are still intact. Its last visit to North Road works was in October 1965, less than two years previously. Arnott Young's scrapyard and its neighbour, the Durham Tube Company, at Fighting Cocks, Dinsdale, have since been obliterated to make way for housing. The track is being singled and cut into small lengths – a procedure that must have cost a fortune in gas.

Class Q6 no. 63371 emerges from the shadow of Darlington North signal-box with a train of sawn timber, March 1963. This robust and simple design proved to be very successful and the last examples were withdrawn at the end of BR steam in north-east England in September 1967 after fifty-four years in service. Each had undergone about twelve major overhauls at North Road (or Gateshead) during this period. The signal-box was one of the largest built by the NER, having 150 levers.

Class V2 no. 60885 takes a heavy mixed freight south near Dalton village. It has just crossed from County Durham into North Yorkshire over the River Tees at Croft, where large-lettered metal signs indicated 'The Border'. The signs were still there at the time of writing, although they are completely obscured from passing trains by dense foliage. They are clearly visible from Middlesbrough FC's training ground as well as from the Croft Working Mens' Club side of the track. The train is approaching the road-bridge leading to the Croft motor-racing circuit in February 1965.

Class Q6 no. 63431, fresh from a visit to North Road works, pictured here at the north end of Bank Top shed on 24 April 1963, pictured during its running-in period before returning to its home shed.

Class V3 no. 67682 working at the north end of Bank Top shed on 5 April 1963. This engine, came to 51A in December 1961 and was withdrawn in September 1963. Its class was never strongly represented at Bank Top shed.

Class J94 no. 68053 passing Cleveland Bridge Engineering Works in May 1963. Darlington's allocation of J94s was about fifteen at most, but there always seemed many more as they were back and forth so many times. Looking now at the new semi-detached houses, neat and tidy roads and lawns it is impossible to believe that a large and famous factory had once occupied the site. After a precarious period in the ownership of Kvaerner, the company now thrives in a new factory on the outskirts of town near Morton Park, after a management buy-out saved it from liquidation. It has also reverted to its original name.

Stanier 2-cylinder 2–6–2T no. 42477, built in 1935, takes a parcels train to Teesside on 15 December 1963. It was transferred to Darlington in December 1961 along with no. 40190 from Wakefield, no. 42085 from York (preserved at the Lakeside & Haverthwaite Railway), no. 42553 from York and no. 42639 from Malton. No. 42477 underwent a general overhaul at North Road works in June 1964, but even so it only lasted another year before being cut up by Drapers at Hull in September 1965. It was officially transferred to 6A Chester in July 1965 and promptly withdrawn. Whether it actually went to Chester is doubtful.

Class A1 no. 60155 *Borderer* awaiting access to works at Bank Top shed for repairs to its accident-damaged cylinder and firebox casing, 27 August 1963. A York engine, it received a boiler change while in the works in September 1963. It remained in service for over two more years, being withdrawn from York in September 1965. Fitted with roller bearings, *Borderer* was considered to be an exceptionally good engine. Several other A1s were fitted with roller bearings, one of which, no. 60154, *Bon Accord*, covered over a million miles in its short life.

Class K1 no. 62001 takes a short freight train north, having just crossed the Stockton & Darlington branch heading for Thompson Street East. The gas-holder on the right is close to the Skerne Bridge, depicted on recent £5 notes commemorating the opening of the Stockton & Darlington to the public on 27 September 1825. The bridge is still used by Bishop Auckland branch line trains, although it stands in an unattractive industrial setting.

The Fighting Cocks crossing and signal-box on the Stockton & Darlington branch, in the summer of 1967. The box is about to be demolished and the track is being singled. The sidings on the right are used by Arnott and Young to store coaches and locomotives prior to scrapping.

No. 63760 was a Class 01 Thompson rebuilt of Robinson's Great Central Railway Class 04. Five were sent to Tyne Dock to assist the Q6s and Q7s with the Consett ore trains. These engines were air-pump-fitted for operating the hopper doors on the ore wagons, as seen here. The other 04s were nos 63712/55 and 63856/74. Along with the Q7s they were displaced by 9Fs and EE Type 3 diesels. After a period in store no. 63760 was sent to Darlington for disposal and is pictured here on the works dead line at Bank Top shed in February 1963.

This 2–6–4 no. 42405 is a Fowler design of 1933 which had been improved by the fitting of cab doors and side-windows. It is crossing from the Down main line heading for shed in July 1963 after transfer from Sowerby Bridge.

Class 9F no. 92148 heads south toward Darlington in August 1964. The houses are on Beaumont Hill on the Great North Road – the main trunk road to Scotland. Darlington was bypassed by the A1M which opened in 1965.

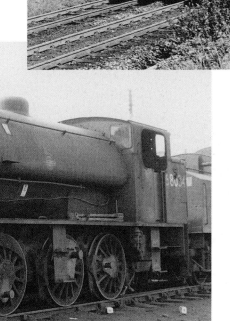

Class J94 no. 68034 from the Cromford & High Peak Railway arrived for scrap on 1 August 1963. It was torched soon afterwards. The C&HPR closed in April 1967, being worked to the end by other J94s which in 1956 displaced the aged North London Tanks of 1879 vintage. Kitson 0–4–0 ST no. 47006 was also tried on the system in 1964. The C&HPR had small sheds at Cromford, Middleton and Sheep Pasture, all under the 17D code as sub-sheds to Rowsley. This engine still carried the old BR emblem and its number was on the bunker, not the saddle tank as was usual. The coupling rods have been sent out on the running plate – not that they will be needed.

BR Standard Class 4MT no. 76050 of West Auckland shed passing McMullen Road level crossing and signal-box, heading east on a mixed freight, on 10 April 1963. This is the original Stockton & Darlington section between North Road station and Oak Tree junction at Middleton St George. At the time McMullen Road was a quiet lane and the trains caused little hindrance to road traffic. The chimneys belong to a brickworks off Arnold Road at the bottom of Hundens Lane. When West Auckland shed closed this engine, together with no. 76049, went to work from Hawick shed on the Waverley route.

Standard Class 4 2–6–0 no. 76050 heading east past McMullen Road level-crossing towards Fighting Cocks. The crossover gave access to Paton & Baldwin's factory from a spur beyond the signal. Paton & Baldwin manufactured woollen products and operated their own fireless locomotive for shooting around the factory yards. The 'boiler' was filled with high-pressure steam from the factory boilers. This fireless locomotive is now preserved in North Road Railway Museum.

Class B1 no. 61382 leaving town past 'Scunny Woods' toward Brafferton on 3 June 1963. A bit of smoke would have enhanced the picture. The B1s constructed at North Road in 1947 produced a couple of landmarks: no. 1020 *Gemsbok* was the works' 2,000th new engine and no. 1029 *Steinbok* was the last LNER engine to be built there.

Class A1 no. 60129 (formerly *Guy Mannering*) at Bank Top shed in June 1965. It is stripped of its name-plates, builder's plate and shed-plate but is still in service. This was the first class A1 to be overhauled at North Road works after Doncaster works had ceased steam repair. Time was almost up for *Guy Mannering*, which was withdrawn from York shed in August. This photograph gives a good view of the 1930s-style shed offices to the right.

Class Q6 no. 63395 passing Darlington Forge and Darlington Wire Mills on the Up slow line on 5 May 1963. A Darlington-based locomotive at this time, it was outshopped from Darlington works for the last time after general overhaul as late as 25 September 1965 and was withdrawn from Sunderland shed (52G) in September 1967, being the last of the class. Steam was eliminated from north-east England with the closure of North Blyth, Sunderland, Tyne Dock and West Hartlepool sheds on 9 September 1967. It is fitting that no. 63395 and class J27 no. 65894, both of NER origin, were active to the end. Both locomotives are preserved in the care of the North East Locomotive Preservation Group.

Class A1 no. 60131 *Osprey* heads south past Bradbury signal-box, 10 June 1964. Several other A1s also carried bird names: no. 60120 *Kittiwake*, no. 60122 *Curlew*, no. 60130 *Kestrel*, no. 60139 *Sea Eagle* and no. 60146 *Peregrine*. New Class A4s carried these names originally but a change in policy meant they had to be renamed. The names were applied to the new A1s several years later.

Class J94 no. 68015 takes a rake of at least eleven tenders of various designs past North Road station to the works or scrapyard, c. 1950. There's not a semaphore signal in sight now. Today this section of platform has been partitioned off and resurfaced as it is used by Bishop Auckland trains. Passengers are not allowed to use the section under the station canopy. (*Geoff Jackson*)

BR Standard Class 2MT no. 78012 at Bank Top on 1 May 1963. After the closure of Northallerton MPD in February 1963 no. 78012 was transferred to Darlington, along with nos 78011, 78014 and 78015 – not that there was work for them all. All sixty-five of these locomotives had been built at Darlington between 1952 and 1956 and were virtually identical to Ivatt's LMS CL 2MT. They were coupled with the BR Class 3 tender, which at 37 tons coaled and watered was the smallest standard type. Bank Top station (originally Central station) was opened in 1887. The Great North of England Railway from York was opened in 1841 and an engine shed built near Albert Hill. This area was eventually surrounded by a maze of lines where the Stockton & Darlington crossed the East Coast Main Line. All the triangles and sidings have gone but the no. 2 road shed remains intact, albeit in very poor condition. The surrounding area is overgrown with trees and bushes, giving little indication of its former complexity (see page 38).

Class A1 no. 60121 *Silurian* with an express freight speeds south past Bank Top station in March 1963. *Silurian* was a York-based engine.

Class J72 no. 69006 reversing towards Bank Top shed which is on the far side of Haughton Bridge in the distance. The location is the Stockton & Darlington crossing and the crossing box can just be seen to the left. Surplus coaches are being stored in the sidings adjacent to the Bishop Auckland branch. The picture was taken on 4 July 1963 and the locomotive was withdrawn in December that year. No. 69006 was one of a batch of fifteen built at North Road in 1949. Five more were built in 1950 and a further eight in 1951. These were all built to the original design by Wilson Worsdell in 1898, half a century earlier. The first of the 'new' Class J72s to be withdrawn was no. 69012 of the 1949 batch from Thornton Junction shed in Scotland.

Peppercorn's Class A1 no. 60141 *Abbotsford* powers away from Darlington's southbound platform no. 1 on 27 March 1963. A York-based engine, it was withdrawn in October 1964.

Class L1 no. 67755, the last of Thompson's class of one hundred locomotives in existence, seen here in the works yard at North Road on 29 June 1963. It was actually withdrawn from Darlington shed in December 1962, but it hung around the works and the scrapyard until the last week in September 1963 when it was finally cut up. As can be seen, it was marked up for urgent attention at North Road. As it took so long to finally dispose of, was it perhaps considered for preservation? The first L1 to be scrapped was no. 67702 in November 1960. The prototype of the class was designed and built at Doncaster works in 1945 and was numbered 9000. The other 99 were produced as follows in 1948–50: Darlington North Road works built 29, Darlington Robert Stephenson's & Hawthorn works built 35, and the North British at Glasgow also built 35. The diesel railcar engines beside the locomotive are waiting to be taken to the old Loco Gear Shop, which had been converted in 1961 for railcar engine overhauls. The author spent several weeks on night shift in this deafening environment as the engines were test-run two at a time for several hours.

Class L1 no. 67777, known as 'the flying sevens', was a long-time Darlington favourite but here it awaits its last short journey from shed to scrapyard on 5 May 1963. It was built by Robert Stephenson's & Hawthorn at their Springfield works about a mile to the north, known locally as 'Stivvies'.

Class J27 no. 65887 behind the old NER roundhouse on the dead line at Bank Top shed. It had been withdrawn from Sunderland shed at the end of May 1963.

Class J94 no. 68025 on the Up slow line approaches the S&D crossing and Haughton Road bridge on 24 April 1963. No. 68025 went for scrap in the following September with two other 51A J94s, nos 68035 and 68040, but replacements arrived in the shape of J94 nos 68008, 68011 and 68059.

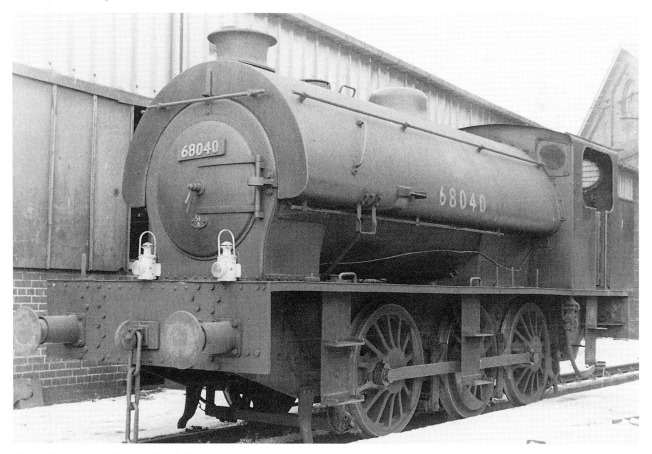

Class J94 no. 68040, the North Road works pilot, parked up for the weekend on a snowy Saturday afternoon in February 1963.

Tyne Dock-based Class 9F no. 92062 waiting to go back to works for further attention after a recent overhaul in February 1960. Tyne Dock received ten of these powerful engines which helped replace the Q7 and 01 classes. No. 92062 was withdrawn from Tyne Dock shed in June 1966.

Ivatt Class 2MT no. 46474 assists at the rear as the train passes the Whessoe factory. The front locomotive will be passing Stooperdale boiler and paint shops, which were annexed from the main works at North Road. To the right is the site of Faverdale wagon works, and one of the buildings can be seen. The NER bought the site from Charles Backhouse for £25,000 in 1913 as it needed to expand its wagon repair and manufacturing capacity in addition to the Shildon facility. It had ready-made links to Shildon works via the original S&D line via Stooperdale Curve.

Cleveland Bridge and Engineering built the works between October 1920 and August 1923 when the first wagons were produced. At its zenith in the mid-1950s it employed 550 workers. It closed on 29 June 1963 on Beeching's recommendation and 366 jobs were lost. Over 150,000 wagons were built or repaired at the site during its forty years of operation. This site is now an industrial estate and employs more people than the works did. Most of the buildings have survived and much new housing has been built to the north. Surrounded by all this development, Faverdale Hall – Charles Backhouse's home when the NER bought the site – still stands, and it is still in use.

Standard Class 4 2–6–4T no. 80076 is from the London, Tilbury & Southend line. The passenger service was operated by a fleet of twenty-seven of these engines, all from Tilbury shed at this time except for one from Shoeburyness. No. 80076 is seen here ex-works passing the site of Carters Row at Bank Top in the spring of 1962.

Another LTS standard, no. 80074, also pictured after a visit to North Road at Bank Top shed a couple of years earlier, on 2 June 1960.

Preserved GWR Castle Class no. 7029 *Clun Castle* at Croft Spa station on clearance tests prior to a special run in August 1967. The EE Type 3 diesel is no. D6834.

A Class WD 2–8–0 heads east on the S&D line across the East Coast Main Line just north of Haughton Bridge, 4 July 1963. The building directly behind the locomotive is the Great North England engine shed, still there today. This apart, the scene is unrecognisable today. The double track in the foreground is the west to north spur connection between the S&D and the main line, opened in about 1861. It was originally known as Ironstone Curve, as it was installed to accommodate ironstone trains from mines in Rosedale on the North Yorkshire Moors to blast furnaces at Ferryhill. These workings went via Picton Junction and Allen's Curve at Eaglescliffe.

A clean Class A4 no. 60034 *Lord Faringdon* speeds south towards Glebe Road bridge in May 1963. This engine joined the stud at Aberdeen Ferryhill shed for its swansong, serving there until September 1966.

Class B1 no. 61403 (or is it 61400?) steamed and waiting to enter service in North Road works yard in 1950. This was one of the last examples built, being from the final batch, nos 61400–9. Was the error rectified before leaving the works? (*Geoff Jackson*)

North Road station in January 1963, long before it housed the present excellent railway museum. Before frequent journeys over the Stainmore line en route to Keswick, the author would obtain a ticket at the dark archaic ticket office. A time-warp even in the early 1960s, it still retains that atmosphere in preservation.

Class J21 no. 65089 double-heads with sister engine no. 65103 into North Road station, possibly with a Blackpool special via Stainmore and Tebay on 18 July 1953. At this time the author was attending Albert Road School, which was situated just behind the signal-box visible through the signal gantry. Today the platform remains intact, including the main nameboard and even the lamppost next to it, although it has an air of neglect with weeds and saplings growing through the flagstone joints. (*Geoff Jackson*)

Standard Class 3MT no. 77000 passes behind North Road station on 1 May 1963. It was a Darlington-based engine at this time. Not the best-looking of the Standard designs, the Class 3MTs were designed and built at Swindon, and only twenty were produced. Another member of the class, no. 77009, was exhibited at the Willesden Exhibition in May 1954, when it was brand new. The engines were allocated equally between North Eastern and Scottish Region sheds. As a class they were the last to suffer any scrap inroads until no. 77010 was withdrawn from Stourton shed (Leeds) in November 1965. No. 77014 left the north when it went to work at Guildford on the Southern Region where it was something of a celebrity. It was the last of the class in service and survived until the curtain came down on Southern Region steam operations in July 1967.

Clan Class Pacific no. 72002 *Clan Campbell* waiting to be scrapped at Darlington on 8 November 1963. Sister engines nos 72000/1/3/4 were nearby awaiting the same fate. Only ten were built, being a lighter version of the very successful Britannias. They were allocated to Carlisle Kingmoor and Polmadie shed in Glasgow but were not considered a success. No. 72002 from Polmadie had been stored at Glasgow Parkhead shed before its final journey after a working life of about ten years. The English-based Clans at Kingmoor survived considerably longer but even they were outlived by some of the Jublilees, Patriots and Royal Scots they were intended to replace.

Class A4 no. 60010 standing in Darlington works yard, stripped of all collectable artefacts, after being withdrawn from Aberdeen Ferryhill shed. Seen here in July 1965, it had arrived under its own steam on 11 May 1965. The Class 8F no. 48689 from Stourton was scrapped but no. 60010 was moved back to Bank Top shed where it stayed until May 1966. After the shed and works closed it was taken to Crewe works where it was cosmetically restored with all the missing parts refitted, then it was sent to Canada for preservation. It was originally named *Woodcock* as LNER no. 4489 and was renamed *Dominion of Canada* in 1937.

Class B1 no. 61275, taking Class V2 no. 60929 to Bank Top shed, passes behind the station in early May 1963. No. 60929 received a general overhaul at North Road works and returned to York shed in June; it survived a further two years before withdrawal in June 1965. No. 61275 returned to York after servicing at Bank Top and was withdrawn in September 1965. Each of the station spans is 60ft high and 1,000ft long, and together they cover an enormous platformed area, with a double bay containing four roads between platforms 1 and 4 at the south end. At the north end there are two separate single bays adjacent to platform 4 outside the canopy, and there is a goods dock at the north end of platform 1.

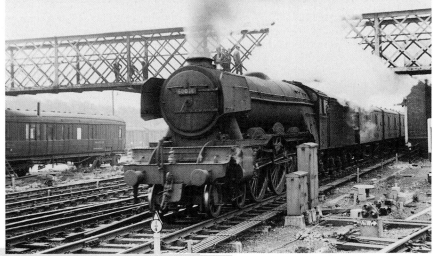

Class A3 Pacific no. 60036 *Colombo* with a Down express parcels train gives Bank Top station a miss as it speeds north in June 1964.

Class A1 no. 60126 *Sir Vincent Raven* of York shed waits to depart south on 7 June 1963. Class V3 no. 67682 has only three months left in service, but still earns a living as station pilot. The tender just edging into the picture belongs to the main line standby engine, Class A3 Pacific no. 60051 *Blink Bonny*.

Class J27 0–6–0s nos 65815 and 65820 leaving their Tyneside depots on 6 June 1963 having been called into the works for overhaul or scrap. They are shown near Beaumont Hill, north of Darlington.

No. 65815 was given a major overhaul and is seen here running in before returning to Tyneside on 20 July 1963. No. 65820 was scrapped.

Preserved Class A3 no. 4472 *Flying Scotsman* southbound near Dalton Village south of Croft Bridge in August 1966. The penultimate A3, no. 60041 *Salmon Trout*, was dismantled at Cowlairs work in Glasgow in July 1966 and the boiler, cylinder and other parts were salvaged for future use on no. 4472.

Class B1 no. 61022 *Sassaby* working hard with a northbound freight passing Green Lane in June 1961. The chimney stack in the distance marks Robert Stephenson's & Hawthorn locomotive works at Springfield.

Class V3 no. 67682 waits at the south end of Bank Top station on 20 July 1963 with three parcels vans, one newly repainted. This engine went to the scrapyard in September 1963.

Class Q7 no. 63460 in Darlington works yard, April 1963. The Q7 0–8–0s were withdrawn in November and December 1962 after an accounting exercise. Many of the class of fifteen were in good working order, having recently been through the works. These were Raven-designed 3-cylinder engines, built at Darlington, five in 1919 and ten in 1924. The whole class was allocated to the Tyne Dock–Consett ore workings, but were displaced by Class 9Fs and EE Type 3 diesels. No. 63460 had been displaced to Thornaby before being called in for scrap and was actually reinstated to traffic to work an enthusiasts' special on 28 September 1963. It is now in the care of the North East Locomotive Preservation Group, based on the North Yorkshire Moors Railway. Ironically the NELPG have acquired the old S&D carriage works in Darlington as a repair base for their engines.

Class V2 2–6–2 no. 60916 in fine condition takes a freight south from Bank Top yard in early May 1963. It had been transferred from Thornaby shed in December 1962, being displaced as dieselisation progressed there.

Class L1 2–6–4T no. 67745 ex-works in June 1960, a long way from its home shed at Hitchin. It returned to Darlington for scrapping in 1963. The closure of many branch lines after the Beeching report and the introduction of diesel rail cars made the class prematurely redundant.

A line of eight Class A8 4–6–2 tanks waiting for the scrapman's torch at Darlington in June 1960. The Class A8s were the last passenger tank design of the NER, being originally built as 4–4–4s. These huge engines weighed in at almost 87 tons. Like their Great Central cousins the Class A5s, they had a high driving position. The cab floorboards can be seen through the narrow doorway on no. 69860.

Standard Class 4 no. 76049 with a mixed freight heading towards Ricknall crossing on the Simpasture branch en route to Teesside on 24 March 1963. No. 76049 was a West Auckland-based engine. The over-bridge in the distance carries the A1 Great North Road through Aycliffe village to Rushyford, now reclassified as the A167.

Class J72 no. 69021 with the departmental engineer's coach passing Darlington south signal-box. With sister engine no. 69022, it was part of the scene around Bank Top for many years. No. 69021 ended its days at West Hartlepool shed in September 1963.

Class K3/2 no. 61927 from Heaton shed, Newcastle, just out of Doncaster works after a general overhaul. It is seen here passing Bank Top station while working its way back home in July 1960.

Class D49/1 4–4–0 no. 62709 *Berwickshire* being cut up at North Road scrapyard in January 1960. The name-plates and builder's plates are still intact. In future years these would have been removed immediately or stolen. The scrapyard was easily accessible as it was enclosed only by low or broken fencing. The class consisted of seventy-six locomotives, all built at Darlington from 1927 to 1935. There were several variations of design, including one rebuilt as an inside-cylinder engine in 1942. This was no. 62768 *The Morpeth*, which was involved in an accident and scrapped in November 1952. They carried the names of the counties through which the LNER operated and those of fox hunts, mainly in northern England; hence the class was referred to as 'hunts' or 'shires'.

Still maintaining some dignity in its final hours, Class J25 no. 65662 will be finished off when the men return after the weekend. Young enthusiasts wander around at will – as did anyone who chose to! June 1960.

Grimy York-based Class V2 no. 60954 with a northbound freight passing Penrose's market garden between Salters Lane and Green Lane in June 1963. The author's home was in Saltersgate Road, just out of the picture, to the right of the greenhouse.

Class A1 no. 60140 *Balmoral* with an easy load of six coaches, June 1963. The distant bridge is Thompson Street East. Salters Lane North bridge spans the last carriage.

Class B1 no. 61032 *Stembok* heads towards Bank Top shed in September 1962. Built in Darlington in August 1947, it lasted until November 1966 and so survived longer than the shed or the works which it last visited in February 1961. The class comprised 410 identical engines built as follows: 60 built at North Road works, delivered from 1942 to 1950; 290 built by the North British Locomotive Co., delivered from April 1946 to April 1952; 10 built by Gorton Works, delivered in 1948 and 1949; and 50 built by the Vulcan Foundry, all delivered in 1947. No. 61057 was scrapped in April 1950 after accidental damage. Other than this one, no. 61085 was the first to be withdrawn in December 1961 – only nine years after the last one emerged from the North British factory in Glasgow.

Class A4 no. 60032 *Gannet* at platform no. 1 on 20 July 1963. Its home shed was New England, Peterborough. It was built in May 1938 as LNER no. 4900. There was to be no Scottish swansong for *Gannet* as it was withdrawn from service three months after this photograph was taken.

A Class V1 rebuilt to a higher boiler pressure became a V3. Here Class V3 no. 67647 from Heaton shed, Newcastle, still looks in reasonable condition at Bank Top shed even though it is on its way to the scrapyard. Some engines were built as V3s.

Class A3 no. 60062 *Minoru* heads south towards Bank Top station between the power station and the shed on 10 July 1963. Built as LNER no. 2561, its double chimney was fitted in 1959 and the Germany-type smoke deflectors in July 1961. It was withdrawn from Peterborough in December 1964 and went to Kings of Norwich for scrapping.

Class A4 no. 60008 *Dwight D. Eisenhower*, relegated to express freight duties, enters platform no. 1 from the north on 8 July 1963. A Peterborough engine, no. 60008 was spared the torch and is now preserved in America. It was originally named *Golden Shuttle* as LNER no. 4496.

A 'Top Shed' engine borrowed by another Top Shed, pictured on 6 June 1960. In other words Darlington Bank Top shed has borrowed Class A4 no. 60015 *Quicksilver* from Kings Cross (34A Top Shed) for main line standby duties. *Quicksilver* was the second built of Gresley's original batch of four for the Silver Jubilee workings.

Class A3 no. 60038 *Firdaussi* approaches platform no. 1 with a train for Leeds on 6 July 1963. The engine is from the city's Neville Hill shed, from where it was withdrawn in November 1963. It was built as LNER no. 2503. By 1963 the station's steam pilots, Class J72s nos 69021 and 69022, had been replaced by diesel shunters.

Class Q6 no. 63357, which has been to works for light repair and to have the valves re-set – the valve settings are chalked on the sand-box. The smokebox door and cylinder covers have been newly painted. The engine's squat powerful lines can be appreciated from this photograph.

Class A3 no. 60070 *Gladiateur* departs from platform no. 4 on 6 August 1963. This is another Neville Hill engine, but its final home was Gateshead shed, and it survived there until May 1964. No. 60070 entered service as LNER no. 2569. Engines trying to start heavy trains from here would often slip very severely when in the charge of less experienced drivers. The spinning wheels and rods, combined with sparks, smoke and steam, made for a sight worth watching as the engine struggled for adhesion.

Class A3 no. 60073 *St Gatien* heads south with a fast freight through the Albert Hill area on 5 May 1963. Only the Up and Down tracks remain here now. The main building belongs to Darlington Forge, which opened in 1853 and closed down in 1967. The Darlington Wire Mills have also closed, although both buildings survive. This engine had only three months left in service. It was the first Pacific to be sent to Darlington works for attention after Doncaster ceased steam work. It was considered to be beyond economic repair and was scrapped in the stripping shop in early September 1963. The Class Q6 on the Up slow is no. 63395, which is now preserved.

Class A3 no. 60064 *Tagalie* travels south light engine under Ketton Bridge on 8 June 1963. There always seemed to be a greater number of northbound passenger trains resulting in engines returning south light. This locomotive was originally named *William Whitelaw* when it was built as LNER no. 2573, but this name was later transferred to Class A4 no. 60004.

Class A3 no. 60084 *Trigo* heads north near Scunny Woods, with Glebe Road bridge in the background, on 26 June 1963. Very little exhaust is visible despite the long uphill gradient from Darlington. Originally LNER no. 2595, it was named *Trigo* after the winner of the 1929 Derby and St Leger races. This engine was withdrawn in November 1964 from Gateshead shed.

Class A1 no. 60126 *Sir Vincent Raven* passing Darlington north signal-box on 10 July 1963. It was named after the Chief Mechanical Engineer of the NER (1910–22), after which date Sir Nigel Gresley became CME of the post-grouping LNER.

Class A1 no. 60124 *Kenilworth*, pictured ex-works with J27 no. 65882 at Bank Top shed on 23 May 1964 before returning to York shed. It was later allocated to Darlington with another Class A1, no. 60145 *Saint Mungo*. No. 60124 was withdrawn when the shed closed on 26 March 1966. Several A1s were named after characters and places from Sir Walter Scott's novels, but sadly none escaped the scrapman's torch.

Class A3 no. 60051 *Blink Bonny* raising steam at Bank Top shed, 17 July 1963. Built as LNER A1 no. 2550, it was rebuilt as an A3 in November 1945. It was allocated to Darlington but finished its service at Gateshead in November 1964. Darlington's main line standby engines were usually a pair of A3s until the A1s took over. Pacifics from other sheds were often borrowed for this duty, including A4s.

Class A1 no. 60131 *Osprey* brings a Down passenger train over Geneva Curve on 27 July 1963. The train was being diverted via Eaglescliffe to Newcastle, either by the east coast route and Sunderland or by the normally freight-only line to Ferryhill where it would rejoin the East Coast Main Line. The name *Osprey* was given to A4 no. 4494 when it was built, but it became *Andrew K. McCosh* in 1942 in honour of an LNER official. There was no *Osprey* until no. 60131 was built at Darlington in September 1948.

Gresley Class V3 no. 67682 takes a couple of Class J94s through North Road station to the scrapyard on 1 May 1963. It would soon make the same journey itself. North Road station on this site dates from 1842. It is now Darlington Railway Museum, although service trains for Bishop Auckland still use the platform behind the name board. The original station dated from 1833 and was situated on the east side of the North Road.

Class A4 no. 60026 *Miles Beevor* coasts south past Ketton, north of Darlington, in June 1963. When it was built as LNER no. 4485 it was named *Kestrel* but was later given the name of an LNER director. Withdrawn from Aberdeen Ferryhill shed in December 1964, it was sent to Crewe works where it was cannibalised to provide spares for another A4, no. 60010 *Dominion of Canada*, before it was dispatched abroad. No. 60026 was not finally finished off until August 1967 when it was sent to the Hughes Bolkow scrapyard at North Blyth, which also demolished A4s nos 60001/24/34.

Thompson-designed B1 no. 61176 raising steam at the north end of Bank Top shed, May 1963. The first B1, LNER no. 8301 (later no. 61000 *Springbok*), was built at Darlington in 1942. It was followed by:

4 in 1943: LNER nos 8302–5 (61001–4)
5 in 1944: LNER nos 8306–10 (61005–9)
5 in 1946: LNER nos 1010–14 (61010–14)
25 in 1947: LNER nos 1015–39 (61015–39)
10 in 1949: BR nos 61350–9
10 in 1950: BR nos 61400–9

Darlington works built 60 of the 410 in total. An unexpected working for this engine occurred on 25 February 1963 when it deputised on the 'North Briton' to Newcastle after a Type 4 diesel failed. On the same day another Darlington B1, no. 61338, had to take the 'Morning Talisman' north at short notice after a Deltic failed. Presumably Darlington's more powerful standby Pacifics and V2s were otherwise engaged. No. 61176 finished its days at York shed in 1965.

Opposite above: Preserved A4 no. 4498 *Sir Nigel Gresley* passing Hopetown signal-box. It is a very different scene now – gone are all the semaphore signals and the signal-box, all the tracks except two for Bishop Auckland (which is single from a few yards further on) and the extensive Whessoe factory have been demolished and replaced by a housing estate.

Opposite below: Class A1 no. 60157 *Great Eastern*, with an Up parcels train, approaching Glebe Road on 12 June 1963. Doncaster-built and Doncaster-based, it remained there until the end of its service in January 1965. It was demolished by Drapers of Hull in early March that year. Nine other A1s also perished there. Several A1s carried the names of constituent LNER companies, including no. 60113 *Great Northern* which was Thompson's 1945 rebuilt A10 (see page 72) and the pioneer A1. The others were no. 60156 *Great Central*, no. 60157 *Great Eastern* and no. 60161 *North British*.

Class K3/3 no. 61871 of 1929 Gresley design, arrived at Bank Top from Hull Dairycoates shed. They were not frequent visitors to North Road works and none was allocated to Bank Top during the 1960s. In all, ninety-two of these engines were built at Darlington from 1924 to 1937. A 3-cylinder 2–6–0 locomotive, it was the precursor of the larger Class V2 2–6–2.

Class A1 no. 60140 *Balmoral* was a York engine borrowed by Bank Top shed to act as main line standby on 17 July 1963. It is waiting in the usual place by the turntable.

Class A1 no. 60121 *Silurian* with an express freight southbound near Bradbury on 8 June 1964. *Silurian* served York shed all its life and ended its days there in September 1965 after only seventeen years service. It was named after the Doncaster Cup winner of 1923.

Darlington's main line standby engine, Class A3 no. 60051 *Blink Bonny*, goes off towards shed on 10 July 1963. Note the mile post showing the distance from York station (44 miles). Darlington main line standby locomotives were usually a pair of A3s at this time, one of which would be parked by the turntable while the other was on shed. They were transferred to and away from 51A in pairs at six-monthly intervals.

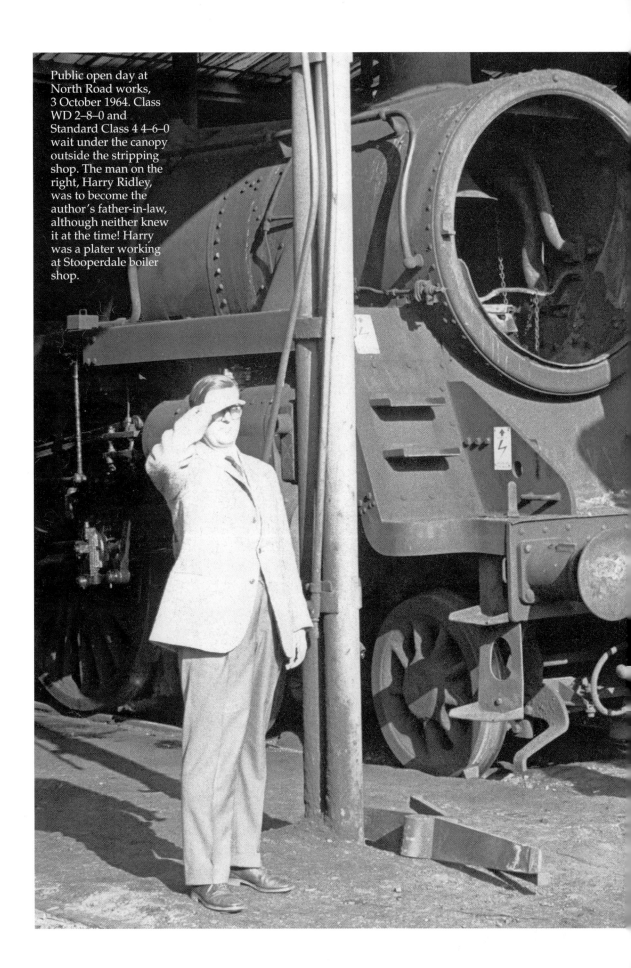

Public open day at North Road works, 3 October 1964. Class WD 2–8–0 and Standard Class 4 4–6–0 wait under the canopy outside the stripping shop. The man on the right, Harry Ridley, was to become the author's father-in-law, although neither knew it at the time! Harry was a plater working at Stooperdale boiler shop.

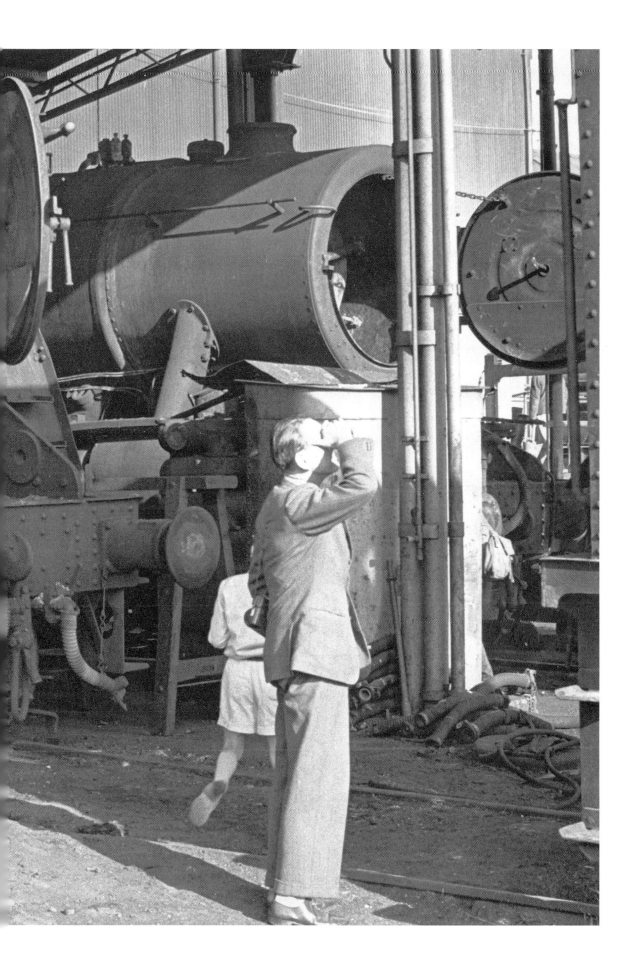

Class A1 no. 60145 *Saint Mungo* passing below the farm road bridge at Ketton with a southbound mixed freight on 12 July 1964. No. 60145 was built at Darlington in 1949 along with ten other A1s. This engine was transferred to Darlington from York in January 1966 and was withdrawn when Bank Top closed on 26 March 1966. However, it was reinstated into service at York shed on 17 April only to be withdrawn finally in June 1966. This engine was the last operational A1 and was scrapped at Drapers of Hull. None of the class was preserved. Peppercorn's class of forty-nine were the last Pacifics designed by one of the big four companies. Pioneer A1 no. 60113 *Great Northern* was developed by Thompson from Gresley's A10s, which in turn were a reclassification of his original A1s of 1922. Peppercorn finalised the design and a further forty-nine were built starting in August 1948 when no. 60114 *W.P. Allen* was delivered, being named after a trade union official. A total of twenty-three were built by North Road works in 1948–9 and a further twenty-six at Doncaster.

Opposite above: A Class A4 by-passes Bank Top station with a Down express in 1959. Neasham Road sidings and goods depot are to the left. The main building still exists, and is used as a milk distribution depot. The other buildings in view belonged to Richardson's Joinery, Simpson's Malt Works and the Cleveland Bridge Engineering Company, they have all been demolished and replaced by a housing estate and supermarket. The lines beneath the signal gantry are holding loops where slow and local workings could wait while faster trains passed through.

Opposite below: Class A3 no. 60042 *Singapore* from 52A Gateshead shed, borrowed this time for main line standby. It was built at Doncaster works in 1934 as LNER no. 2547 and was named after the winner of the 1930 St Leger. It finished its days in Scotland, being withdrawn from St Margarets shed, Edinburgh, in July 1964. It is seen here in its original Class A3 condition having a single chimney, no deflectors and a Great Northern tender.

Engines bask in the warm afternoon sunshine on a quiet Sunday in June 1964. Darlington works built thirty-seven of these Derby-designed LMS types in 1950–1 including this one, no. 43102, which was allocated here at this time.

A much better view with the boiler and chimney behind. The driver of Class J94 no. 68071 looks very comfortable as a few trucks are taken to Croft yard in July 1964.

Class B1 no. 61322 heads north with a freight on a wet day in May 1964. It is pictured emerging from the back of Bank Top station after being held in the goods loop. The front end of a single front wheel goods delivery truck can be seen in Neasham Road goods depot.

Class B1 no. 61032 *Stembok* and K1 no. 62050, both surplus to requirements, pictured at the south end of Bank Top shed in June 1964. St John's Church is in the distance.

Class A3 no. 60111 *Enterprise* from 34F (Grantham shed), borrowed for standby duties in May 1961. Built as LNER no. 4480, it was named after the 1887 2,000 Guineas winner. Here, waiting beside the turntable at Bank Top shed, no. 60111 is fitted with a double chimney and is coupled to an LNER straight-sided tender, but it failed to acquire the German-type smoke deflectors before being withdrawn from Grantham shed in December 1962.

Class A3 no. 60040 *Cameronian* by the buffer stops just off the turntable at Bank Top in July 1960. Its final abode was Gateshead shed (52A) where it survived until June 1964. It was originally built as LNER no. 2505. The Class A3 engines were developed from Gresley's A1 Pacifics. Rebuilding began in 1928 and the original A1s were reclassified as A10 until conversion to Class A3 was complete. No. 60040 is fitted with a double chimney and is coupled to a Great Northern railed tender; it was later fitted with German-type smoke deflectors.

Class WD 2–8–0 no. 90370 receives final adjustments outside the weighing shed at North Road works on 25 April 1964. The Ministry of Supply began ordering these engines in 1943 to a design by R.A. Riddles. They were bought by BR in 1948, being surplus to military requirements when the war ended. North British built 422 engines which BR numbered 90000–421. Vulcan Foundry built 311 engines which BR numbered 90422–732. The last engine, no. 90732, was named *Vulcan* and was the only one of the class to have a name.

No. 90639 at Bank Top shed waiting its call to works on 5 April 1963. The circle underneath the cab-side number indicates that the engine is one of Wakefield's (56A) best, being used on bonus-earning coal trains. No. 90639 was torched by Butlers of Otley in early August 1964, only fourteen months after its last general overhaul at Darlington. Drapers of Hull were the greediest consumer of WDs, eating through 205 of the 733 2–8–0s built. Darlington saw off just 47.

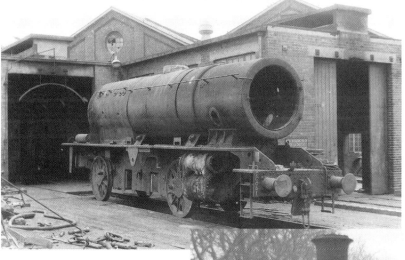

The bare bones of WD no. 90061 beside the steaming shed at North Road works. The class were crudely and simply built but were very effective. 935 were built in total, 545 by the North British Locomotive Company and 390 by the Vulcan Foundry. 733 were purchased by British Railways, leaving 202 overseas or destroyed.

Class J77 0–6–0T no. 68406 at North Road scrapyard in 1958. The J77s were built originally as 0–4–4Ts as NER Class 290 in 1874, to Edward Fletcher's design, and rebuilt by Wilson Worsdell beginning in 1899 as 0–6–0Ts, some at York and some at Darlington. The York rebuilds retained the rounded cab features, as on no. 68406, while Darlington rebuilt with square cabs. The class became extinct during 1960.

Class WD no. 90082 heading south over Yarm Road bridge with a train of ore wagons in April 1964. The 733 Austerity 2–8–0s purchased by British Railways were distributed as follows: London Midland region – 261, Eastern region – 260, North Eastern region – 109, Scottish region – 54, Western region – 49. The Southern region did not get any. The entire class of twenty-five larger 2–10–0 WD engines was allocated to the Scottish region. Many other engines of these classes were sent overseas during the war and many continued in service abroad after 1945.

Class A4 no. 60017 *Silver Fox*, relegated to freight workings in April 1963, taking a load of empty tank wagons south on the Up slow line past Bank Top station. Worse was to come for *Silver Fox* as it was taken out of service from Peterborough shed in October 1963. A batch of four locomotives emerged from Doncaster works between September and December 1935, all with *Silver* in their names, and intended to work the Silver Jubilee expresses. They were LNER no. 2509 *Silver Link*, no. 2510 *Quicksilver*, no. 2511 *Silver King* and no. 2512 *Silver Fox*. The silver fox emblem can be seen on the side of the engine. The first A4s to be withdrawn, numbered 60003/14/28/30/33, all from Kings Cross shed, went in December 1962. No. 60017 was one of eleven cleared out at about the same time and sent to Peterborough New England shed.

A Class V2, No. 60884, approaching Salters Lane North bridge with a long train of mixed freight and parcel vans in March 1965. The bridge in the distance is Thompson Street East and the long building behind is Darlington Forge. The tall chimneys of course belong to Darlington power station. At Thompson Street the double track increased to three with the Up slow diverging here. There was also a crossover from the Down to the Up main for access to Robert Stephenson's & Hawthorn works. The area was controlled by a signal-box on the Up side just south of the bridge. There were two freight derailments here in the 1950s.

Ivatt Class 4MT no. 43057, recently transferred to Darlington from Thornaby, approaching Glebe Road bridge from the north on 5 June 1963. The train is made up of a mixture of old timber and steel coal-wagons.

Departmental Locomotive no. 54 waiting for the torch at North Road scrapyard in June 1961. This engine was based at the Permanent Way Reclamation Depot at Geneva Road and its previous BR number 68153, is still on the cab front. Designed by the Sentinel Wagon Co., it was built in 1933 under British Railways classification Y1/2. A similar engine, no. 53 (BR no. 68152), was based at Faverdale wagon works, but this was classified Y1/1. Fortunately no. 54 was purchased by the Middleton Railway Preservation Society and can still be seen in working order at their line in Leeds.

Class A8 no. 69874 from Sunderland Shed waits outside the stripping shop at North Road works on 5 June 1960. But instead of another general overhaul it was sent over the road for scrapping.

Standard Class 5 4–6–0 no. 73168 crosses from the Down main over to the shed in March 1963 before a visit to the works. Class 5 engines were seldom seen at Darlington except for works visits.

Standard Class 4 4–6–0 no. 75052 waiting on the works line at Bank Top in November 1964. It was another rare visitor as none was allocated to North Eastern sheds, but in the winter of 1963/4 there was an influx of these engines for repair at North Road shops, mainly from LMR sheds but two or three from the Western region. These were returned to the Western in green livery and fully lined out.

Class Q1 0–8–0T no. 69934 from Frodingham shed, called in for scrapping in 1959. These engines were distributed between Selby, Frodingham and Langwith Junction and were used on hump and heavy shunting duties. These were not North Eastern engines but rebuilds of Robinson's Q4 of Great Central Railway origin.

Class J73 no. 68364 from West Hartlepool shed photographed at Bank top in June 1960 en route to the scrapyard. This Wilson Worsdell design of 1891 was the NER's largest 0–6–0T, and was fitted with a J24 boiler. The final engine in the class was no. 68361, which was cut up at Darlington in November 1960.

LNER Class N10 0–6–2T no. 69097 at the scrapyard on 7 September 1962 alongside the original S&D carriage works, now the home of the new Class A1 'Tornado' project. Along with sister N10s nos 69101 and 69109, this engine worked the Bowes/Marley Hill Colliery railways until being withdrawn on 9 April 1962. They were the last of the NER 0–6–2Ts, designed in 1902 by Wilson Worsdell. Twenty were built at Darlington works as NER Class U. These were large tank engines with a boiler that was interchangeable with several other classes, including the J21 tender engines. As no class A1 Pacifics were preserved, the A1 'Tornado' project will create a new mainline locomotive basically to Peppercorn's original design but using modern materials and engineering methods. It will be numbered 60163 and named *Tornado*.

Class V2 2–6–2 no. 60884 approaching Haughton Bridge on the Up slow in June 1964. The building on the left is Darlington Forge. A Darlington-based engine, it was returning to shed after taking a freight north.

Class V2 no. 60929 of York shed heading home just north of Darlington in June 1964. The houses in the distance are on Beaumont Hill on the Great North Road.

Standard Class 4 2–6–0 no. 76020 from 5F Uttoxeter shed undergoes minor repairs in the works yard on 3 October 1964. This engine was originally allocated to Kirby Stephen, on the Stainmore line, when it was new in 1954.

Fairburn tank no. 42085, still wearing a York shed-plate, with the NER directors' saloon in June 1962. Alongside is A4 no. 60006 *Sir Ralph Wedgwood* from Kings Cross shed, waiting with a rake of passenger coaches which were being run in after undergoing repairs at York carriage works. The original *Sir Ralph Wedgwood* was destroyed by a German bomb at York in April 1942. No. 60006 was originally named *Herring Gull*.

Class A1 no. 60127 *Wilson Worsdell* has arrived at Bank Top platform No. 1 with a passenger train to complete a rare line-up with nos 42085 and 60006 in June 1962.

Class Q6 no. 63389 from Tyne Dock shed, heading south with a van, passes the S&D crossing in early 1964. To the left of the buffer beam is a sign indicating the original S&D route. The building behind the sign is Summerson's Foundry.

Class B1 4–6–0 no. 61337 of York shed (50A) brings a freight north through Haughton Bridge on an October morning in 1964. Note the unusual low-roofed vans in the consist. The private house on the right was probably occupied by a railway man as there is a gap in the wall giving access directly from the garden to the tracks.

With Horwich works already closed and Doncaster and Derby works no longer engaged on steam repairs, the doomed Darlington plant dealt with several classes that would not previously have been repaired there. Here two Class 8Fs, nos 48711 and 48722, wait outside the stripping shop at North Road works with Class B1 no. 61303 on 3 October 1964.

All three locomotives were repaired and returned to service. No. 48722 from Speke Junction in Liverpool is fitted with a small Fowler LMS railed tender.

Class B1 no. 61303 awaiting its fate outside the stripping shop on 3 October 1964. It was overhauled and returned to its home shed at York in early December.

Darlington Class V2 no. 60806 gets a rub-down at Bank Top shed in August 1965. The mutilated *Dominion of Canada* awaits its fate with Class WD no. 90430 in the background. No. 60806 arrived at Darlington in June 1964 to replace withdrawn V2 no. 60809 *The Snapper*.

Class V3 no. 67665 on the executioner's block at Darlington scrapyard in July 1961. It seems to have been partially cleaned up for the event.

Class A1 no. 60145 *Saint Mungo* undergoes light repairs at North Road in October 1964. This engine was stored out of work at Hull Dairycoates earlier in the year. It was returned to service and survived to be the last of its class.

Class A3 no. 60052 *Prince Palatine* stands by at Bank Top on 27 July 1963. It went on to be the last survivor of the class, being withdrawn from St Margarets shed in Edinburgh in January 1966.

Class A3 no. 60058 *Blair Atholl* stands by in August 1962. There was less than a year to go for this engine. It was transferred to Heaton shed, Newcastle, and finished there in June 1963. The main building to the right of the engine is the Railway Plant & Foundry, long since demolished and replaced by houses.

Class A1 no. 60140 *Balmoral* from York shed taking a fast freight north from Darlington in May 1964.

Class V2 no. 60877, another York-based engine, with an express parcels on the same day.

Class A1 no. 60116 *Hal o' the Wynd* takes coal empties north having just passed Glebe Road bridge in May 1964. No. 60116 was working from Tweedmouth shed (52D) at the time and still had another twelve months left in service before it was withdrawn from Gateshead shed.

Class A1 no. 60140 *Balmoral* pilots a Class A3 back to York or Darlington. Class V2 no. 60884 is on the slow line heading for shed and is just passing the S&D crossing. The section of S&D between here and McMullen Road crossing was closed on 21 May 1967. Paton & Baldwin's factory could still be accessed by the remaining single line section from Oak Tree Junction. This section lasted another ten years; it closed in 1977 and the track was removed the following year.

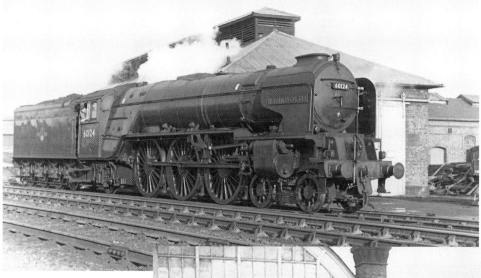

Class A1 no. 60124 *Kenilworth* passing the old Great North of England engine shed near the S&D crossing in June 1964. A York engine, it was running-in after a visit to North Road works for what proved to be its last major repair. No. 60124 later returned to Bank Top shed and finished its days there in March 1966.

Class A2 no. 60539 *Bronzino* from Heaton shed, Newcastle, waits to depart from platform no. 1 at Bank Top station in March 1962. No. 60539 was a Peppercorn 1947 version of the earlier A2/2 and was fitted with a double chimney. It was scrapped at Doncaster works in May 1963.

A rare LMS visitor, Black Five Class 5MT 4–6–0 45204 from Farnley Junction shed, Leeds, heading north towards Brafferton in July 1964. This was a Sunday working which usually produced a Class Black Five or a Jubilee.

Class A1 no. 60131 *Osprey* with a Down freight north of Darlington in June 1964. No. 60131 was based at 55A Leeds Holbeck shed. More and more Pacifics were being relegated to freight duties as main line diesels increasingly displaced them from express passenger work.

Class WDs nos 90016 and 90014 receive attention at Bank Top repair shops. Everything is kept clean and tidy despite there being only six months to closure. The coupling and connecting rods are ready to be refitted.

Class V2 no. 60810 takes a mixed freight north towards Brafferton in June 1964.

Class A3 no. 60036 *Colombo* brings an Up passenger train beneath the farm bridge at Ketton. *Colombo* came to Bank Top shed in December 1963 with classmate no. 60045 *Lemberg* to take over main line standby duties. The previous incumbents, no. 60051 *Blink Bonny* and no. 60075 *St Frusquin* moved on to Gateshead shed. *Colombo* and *Lemberg* were the last of a long sequence of A3s assigned to this duty since they took over from the Class C7 Atlantics in 1948. Both A3s were scrapped at Darlington in November 1964. Class A1 no. 60124 *Kenilworth* was transferred from York shed as a replacement, reinforced later by another A1, no. 60145 *Saint Mungo*. Between them they covered the last fifteen months until the shed closed in March 1966. No. 60124 was withdrawn but no. 60145 was reprieved for another three months' service at York. They were both scrapped at Drapers of Hull.

Class A3 no. 60045 *Lemberg* stands by at Darlington shed on 12 August 1964. This was *Lemberg*'s last home, as it was withdrawn on 21 November 1964. Along with classmate no. 60036 *Colombo*, it was in service on standby duty right up to that evening and was broken up at Darlington soon afterwards. Built as LNER no. 2544, it was named after the Derby and Doncaster Cup winner of 1910.

Extract from the *Railway Observer*, 1963: 'On Xmas Eve of 1962 "Lemberg" deputised for a failed diesel for Newcastle to Liverpool express. It spent Xmas Day in Liverpool and then on Boxing Day double-headed a Liverpool to York mail as far as Leeds, then worked a Leeds to Glasgow express the next day.' It just shows how difficult it could be for a shed master to get his engine back!

Class A3 no. 60112 *St Simon* heading south towards Darlington. The wooded area to the right is referred to on the map as Skerneingham, but is known locally as Scunny Woods. Hidden in a thicket here is a large depression in the ground said to have been used for cock-fighting in days gone by. No. 60112 was one of the longest-lived A3s, being withdrawn in December 1964 after forty-one years in service. It was named after the 1885 Ascot Gold Cup winner.

Bank Top-based Class WD no. 90014 takes the west to south spur off the S&D towards Bank Top yards and Haughton Bridge, in March 1964. It is passing through Jolly's second-hand timber yard, which mainly sold old sleepers. Note the old passenger coach used as the yard's office.

Class K1 no. 62044 heading north past Aycliffe village with a short train of flat wagons in July 1964.

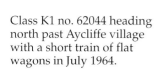

Class V2 no. 60810 waits in the loop at Aycliffe village in June 1965 for permission to return to its home depot at York after taking a train of tanker wagons to Ferryhill. This engine lasted only five more months.

Darlington-based Class K1 no. 62001 heading north in May 1964 with a train of tanker wagons. Note the two trucks acting as a buffer between the locomotive and the potentially hazardous chemicals in the tanks.

Heading back to base at Darlington, this is Class K1 no. 62044 near Aycliffe village in July 1964.

Class K1s nos 62045 and 62059 at Bank Top shed awaiting their next turns in June 1964. K1s were the mainstay of Darlington's medium-distance freights right up to closure on 26 March 1966.

Class A1 no. 60155 *Borderer* returns south to its home shed at York past Scunny Woods north of Darlington in late September 1963, not long after a visit to North Road works.

Class A1 no. 60128 *Bongrace* brings an express south through Ketton bridge near Aycliffe in June 1963. To judge by the smokebox number-plate it may have been mistaken for no. 60123, which had been scrapped some time earlier.

Class K1 no. 62059 heads south towards Darlington in November 1965, photographed from Glebe Road bridge. Scunny Woods show up well against the snow. The public footpath to the woods and beyond can be seen running parallel to the fence on the right.

North Road scrapyard from the cab of a condemmed class A8 in July 1960. A large wheel lathe from North Road works also awaits the torch. The works had renewed some of its older machinery at this time. Engines were cut up here from 1932 to 1964, after which they were dismantled in the works or went to private scrapyards. The buildings in view were the Kitching & Lister Foundries which built engines for the S&D; *Locomotion No. 1* was exhibited there from 1857 to 1892. Sadly these buildings have gone.

Opposite above: Class J94 no. 68038 ex-works for the last time before being returned to Blaydon shed on 21 February 1960. It was withdrawn from Tyne Dock shed in November 1963. It wouldn't have remained in this immaculate condition for more than a few days. Shed cleaners didn't waste elbow grease on J94 shunters.

Opposite below: Class J94 no. 68060 scuttles for the umpteenth time past the north end of Bank Top station on 15 May 1963. R.A. Riddles modified Hunsley Engine Company's standard 0–6–0 saddle tank shunter design before 377 were ordered by the Ministry of Supply. Several companies contributed to the building programme. Apart from the 75 sold to British Railways, they were aquired by many colleries and industrial complexes throughout the country.

Class D49/2 no. 62740 *The Bedale*, called in for scrap, pictured at Whessoe crossing with Class 9F no. 92178 which was waiting to go into works, as a new Sulzer Type 2 diesel no. D5105, receives final adjustments in May 1960. Sulzer engineers from Switzerland were permanently seconded to the works. The old NER engine shed was used as a test-house for the diesels and is still in industrial use today.

Ex-Crosti Class 9F 2–10–0 no. 92025 brings a cattle train from behind Bank Top station in May 1964. The train crossed all the lines in view and reversed into Neasham Road goods depot seen opposite. The locomotive is from Wellingborough shed (15A) and was the only ex-Crosti seen at Darlington by the author.

Flagship Class V2 no. 60800 *Green Arrow* from Kings Cross shed waiting to enter the works at Bank Top shed in May 1961. 'Green Arrow' was the name given to an LNER parcels service. No. 60800 is the only example of Gresley's class of 184 to be preserved, being part of the National Collection at York. At the time of writing, it has been fully restored and is working main line specials.

Class V2 no. 60855 at Bank Top platform no. 4 with train no. 58 in July 1962. The DMU for Barnard Castle waits alongside while the Crook DMU is in the bay platform. Apart from the main through line this area has been filled in and is now used for car parking.

A Class K1 storms south past the Cleveland Bridge Engineering works in December 1962. The site is now a housing estate and the only indications of the previous engineering activity are the rail lines set into Smithfield Road approaching the narrow underpass.

Class Q6 no. 63341 of West Auckland shed heads west at Ricknall crossing on 23 April 1963. It finished its days at West Hartlepool shed (51C) in November 1964. The building in view is the disused electric sub-station which served the line when it was electrified from Shildon to Newport. In 1914 ten electric freight engines were built at North Road works. The line reverted to steam working in 1935 as coal traffic declined and investment in new electrical equipment could not be justified. There were plans to electrify the East Coast Main Line and in May 1922 an experimental electric passenger locomotive designed by Sir Vincent Raven emerged from the works. Described as a 4–6–4, it underwent initial testing on this line but, with the Grouping of 1923 imminent, the electrification scheme was shelved and the engine went into store in Stooperdale paint shop until 1950 when it was cut up.

Opposite above: West Auckland class Q6 no. 63344, seen here at Ricknall crossing on 5 April 1963, was called into works in July 1963 for a general overhaul. The continuation of the crossing road can be seen above the gatepost; it crosses the East Coast Main Line there, which passes below the branch line a few yards to the north. The old sub-station has been demolished and a modern electricity sub-station now marks the site. Nothing but dense bushes can be seen from this location today. The signals protecting the crossing were operated from a ground frame in a cabin close by and the gates were opened and closed by the crossing keeper.

Opposite below: Class J94 no. 68050, one of Darlington's ubiquitous saddle-tank shunters, passing under the open structured foot-bridge on 15 August 1963. At one time the foot-bridge spanned all the lines and linked Neasham Road to the back of Pensbury Street behind platform no. 4. The section spanning the station approach and platform no. 4 was later demolished and never replaced. The section shown here was replaced with the awful concrete and plastic structure there today. No. 68050 lasted until the end of November 1964.

Class J94 no. 68043 heads towards Croft yard with a mixed train of coal-wagons and covered vans on 5 April 1963. The cleared land in the foreground fronted Carters Row, a line of terraced houses whose windows opened directly on to the tracks. The long timbers are new sleepers ready to be placed under the full span of the crossovers. No. 68043 stayed at 51A until it was withdrawn in May 1965.

The forlorn remains of a Class B16 at the snow-covered North Road scrapyard in February 1963. The first engine to be cut up on this site was a D17 4–4–0 from Alnmouth shed which arrived on 28 October 1932. Ivatt Atlantics, Raven Pacifics, Gresley Pacifics and V2s, most NER classes, BR Standards and locomotives of LMS origin all met their end here. The scrapyard closed officially in mid-March 1964 although there was sporadic activity after that date as the works stripping shop became short of space. The last locomotive to be cut up was Class J94 no. 68039, an insignficant little engine compared with the large and historic locomotives that preceded it. The entire area has now been covered with topsoil and grassed over. Who knows what still lurks beneath.

A strong westerly wind drives the steam from the coolers across Bank Top shed in February 1963. Class WD nos 90082 and 90430 are in the line of dead engines. The steam from the coolers often created its own mini-climate in Borough Road and the surrounding streets. Rain and drizzle would dampen the local area while the weather all around was fine. The power station was Darlington's major landmark, being visible from miles around. It was built in 1935 and demolished soon after closure in 1978.

Class K1 no. 62008 returns to base with Darlington's steam crane breakdown set in April 1965. This was housed in a specially built shed at Bank Top adjacent to the round-house.

Inside Bank Top repair shops in August 1965, with Class WD no. 90011 receiving attention and Ivatt Class 4 no. 43129 looking in. Closure would follow just seven months later.

Class K1 no. 62008 heading north with a short freight passing Bank Top station on 3 May 1965. The K1s were developed by Thompson (and later Peppercorn) from Gresley's successful K4s designed specifically for the West Highland line. The K1s eventually displaced the K4s, first to Thornton Junction shed then to the scrapyard in 1961. Fortunately one K4 is preserved, no. 61994 *The Great Marquess*, as is K1 no. 62005 which returned to the former stamping-grounds of its sister engines, the Fort William to Mallaig line, for summer steam workings.

Ex-LMS 2–6–4T no. 42477 at Bank Top on 5 April 1963. This is Stanier's 1935 version of this ubiquitous type of passenger tank engine. No. 42477 was transferred to Darlington after the closure of Malton shed.

Ex-LMS 2–6–4T no. 42194 coaling up at Darlington on 13 June 1965. A Fairburn development of Stanier's design, it was built at Derby works in 1948 and delivered new to Corkerhill (67A) shed in Glasgow. It remained in south-west Scotland until October 1964 when it was transferred to Wakefield (56A) and then to Darlington in November 1964, from where it was withdrawn in August 1965.

Class J27 no. 65860 backs off shed in June 1962 at the north end of Bank Top station. DMUs for Crook and Barnard Castle are waiting in the north bay platforms. This engine was later fitted with a snowplough and was one of the last to leave 51A after the shed closed. It was removed in the summer of 1966 to North Blyth where it was placed in store and then transferred to Sunderland when the last Class J27s were cleared out. It was withdrawn from there in May 1967.

Ivatt Class 2MTs nos 46474 and 46475 struggle with a heavy train, which includes seven large steel pipes, around Hopetown curve and on to the Barnard Castle branch. Hopetown signal-box is obscured. The pipes were for a water pipeline being laid in Teesdale in about 1960. Darlington built thirty-eight examples of this class but not these two.

A Black Five, a very rare visitor to Darlington, heads north with a freight between the cooling towers and shed in 1960. This photographer would have been standing on a bike seat as the sandstone wall was too high to see over without assistance!

Class V2 no. 60962 from Heaton shed, shown as built with inside steam pipes and single chimney, 20 July 1963. Some engines were later fitted with outside steam pipes which made them look very similar to the A3s. A few were also fitted experimentally with double chimneys. As usual, the south end of platform no. 1 was busy with spotters of all ages. No. 60960 was the first North-Eastern-based V2 to go, being cut up at Darlington in March 1962, while no. 60977 was the first of the class of 184 to be scrapped, after an accident at Walton Wood earlier the same month.

A quiet Saturday afternoon in the works yard on 9 April 1960. Class J94 works shunters nos 68008 and 68045 are at rest with a Class B1 and a J27. North Road works was opened in 1863 by the NER and closed in February 1966. It covered 27 acres and employed 3,500 men at its peak. The last engine to receive attention was Standard Class 4 no. 76040, but the repairs were not completed and it left the works on 3 February and was taken to Crewe works with a couple of scrap Class 8Fs. Crewe was expected to deal with ex-NER engines after Darlington closed but none was sent there: they were either repaired in the north-east or scrapped.

Class V2 no. 60856 from York shed heading home from platform no. 1 with an eight-coach passenger train, on 27 July 1963. Such a train was well within the V2's capabilities as they were known to have lifted over twenty coaches during the Second World War. This engine has been fitted with outside steam pipes.

Class 9F 2–10–0 no. 92179 from New England shed, Peterborough, running-in after a visit to North Road. Class J72 no. 69022, one of the station pilots, was built at Darlington as one of the late batch of 1951 to Wilson Worsdell's design of 1898. Almost the full span of the old station foot-bridge can be seen in this view, taken on 6 June 1961. This 9F was destroyed at the Hughes Bolkow scrapyard, North Blyth, in July 1966, after just seven years in service. Its last home (for eleven months) was Colwick shed, Nottingham, where it was declared surplus to requirements in November 1965.

Class V2 no. 60895 takes its train of coal-wagons out of the holding loop behind Bank Top station on 7 July 1964 as Class J94 no. 68025 hurries away in the opposite direction. Bank Top station was opened in 1887, having been designed by William Bell for the North Eastern Railway Company. The S&D route lost its passenger traffic at this time when a new link opened from Bank Top station to Oak Tree Junction at Middleton St George. The original S&D stretch from Albert Hill survived as a through route for goods traffic, diversions and excursions until it was severed on 21 May 1967. The new station, originally named Central, cost the NER £110,000. Although it was widely known as Bank Top that name appeared on the station's name boards only for a brief period in 1948–9.

Opposite above: Class WD no. 90357, with a Gateshead-based English Electric Type 4 diesel (no. D248) and a brake van behind, takes water at Parkside in March 1963. Its destination was probably further north otherwise it would have filled up at shed. Perhaps no. D248 had failed and was being taken home. One of the crew can be seen attending to the water bag.

Opposite below: Class A3 no. 60100 *Spearmint* at North Road in June 1965. It was scheduled for general overhaul but was found to have a badly cracked frame. Built as LNER no 2796, it was named after the 1906 Derby winner. It was built at Doncaster works in 1930 and spent all its life at Scottish sheds. Class 8F no. 48689 was also scrapped and Jinty no. 47564 was out-shopped as a stationary boiler without cab or tanks, painted black but unnumbered. The first A3 to go was no. 60104 *Solario* from Kings Cross shed in December 1959, and by the end of 1964 only 3 of the 78 total remained in service. No. 60100 was one of them. The others were nos 60041 and 60052, the latter being the last to go in January 1966 from St Margarets shed, Edinburgh. Nine A3s were scrapped at Darlington.

Class 8F no. 48381 ex-works at Bank Top shed in June 1965. Another 8F, no. 48329, is on the left. Darlington works began to repair 8Fs after Horwich works closed on 6 May 1964. The last engine overhauled there was no. 48756 from Carlisle Kingmoor shed.

Class 8Fs, Ivatt Class 4s and various Standard classes make 51A look more like an LMR shed in 1964/5 as foreign engines visited North Road works and then were prepared at Bank Top shed before returning home. The three Class 8Fs and the Ivatt Class 4 illustrate the point, although the Ivatt belonged to 51A in June 1965.

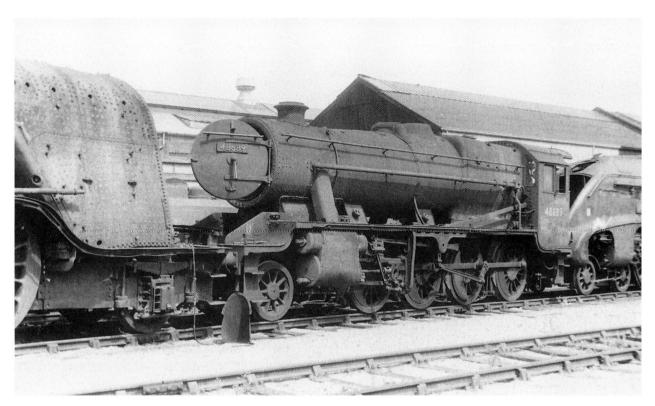

Class 8F no. 48689 from Stourton shed, Leeds, in the works yard in June 1965, flanked by two LNER Pacifics – Class A3 no. 60100 *Spearmint* and Class A4 no. 60010 *Dominion of Canada*. All three had been condemned. Happily the A4 was spared the torch and now resides in Vancouver Museum, Canada.

Class 8F no. 48100 waits for its paintwork to be completed after the refitting of the boiler cladding at North Road in 1965. Alongside is the tender of an overhauled Class WD and the body shell of a new Sulzer Class 2 diesel. North Road works built forty-three of these Stainer-designed LMS engines: thirteen in 1944, seventeen in 1945 and thirteen more in 1946.

Class A4 no. 60023 *Golden Eagle* at Bank Top shed on 15 July 1963, displaying a Gateshead shed-plate. It was transferred to Edinburgh St Margarets shed in November 1963 and then to Aberdeen Ferryhill in June 1964 after a period in store at Bathgate. It joined a stud of other A4s assembled there to work the Aberdeen–Glasgow three hour expresses. Unfortunately it didn't reign long there, being withdrawn in November 1964. Other A4s displaced to Scotland from English sheds included nos 60004/5/6/7/9/10/12/16/19/26/31. Four of these, nos 60007/9/10/19, are preserved. No. 60023 was built as LNER no. 4482 at Doncaster works in 1936, being the first of a batch of five turned out in green livery.

Class J39/1 no. 64868 stands in the cold during its final hours at North Road scrapyard in January 1963. All 289 locomotives of this class were identical, although they were coupled to tenders of various capacities.

Darlington-based Class B1 no. 61321 with a southbound goods train approaching Glebe Road bridge in April 1964.

Class A4 no. 4498 *Sir Nigel Gresley* whistles through Croft Spa station in July 1966. The wooden steps are for passengers using the Richmond branch DMUs. The station platforms were demolished by explosives on a Sunday morning after the Richmond branch closed in March 1969. The stationmaster's sign was displayed in the bar of the nearby Station Hotel and a Croft Spa totem is owned by a local resident. In a nearby garden the main tangerine name board is visible, although damaged.

BR Standard Class 4 no. 76050 from West Auckland shed heads east towards Ricknall crossing and Teesside on the Simpasture branch on 5 April 1963, having just passed Aycliffe trading estate before the A1 over-bridge.

Darlington-based Class V2 no. 60809 *The Snapper* heading for home near Dalton village in April 1964. No. 60809 came to Bank Top shed from Heaton in June 1961 and its last major overhaul at North Road was in November 1960. It was withdrawn in June 1964. In exchange, 51A received two V2s, nos 60806 and 60884.

The engine's full name was *The Snapper, The East Yorkshire Regiment, The Duke of York's Own*.

Class A1 no. 60128 *Bongrace* leaves Ferryhill station for Darlington in July 1964. This station closed on 6 March 1967 and now there are no traces of the semaphore signals, station or signal-box.

Class J50/1 no. 68898, of Great Northern Railway origin, came to Darlington from Bradford in 1959. Designed by Gresley, the class was built from 1922 to 1937. A rare visitor to true North Eastern territory, it lasted only a few months at Darlington. Here it pushes flat wagons on the spur leading to the Railway Plant and Foundry. As can be seen, the spur into the foundry had a very short head shunt before buffering up to the round-house, so only a couple of trucks could be shunted at a time. Again, the 1930s-style bay windows of the shed offices can be appreciated, seen from the opposite side to the view shown on page 108.

Two Class V2s wait on the works line at Bank Top in December 1962. No. 60825 from St Margarets shed, Edinburgh, received a general overhaul and was sent home in January 1963.

Class K1 no. 62056 coasts downhill to Croft viaduct near Dalton village with coal empties in September 1964. The handrails on each embankment mark the route of a public footpath.

Class J21 nos 65099 and 65033 withdrawn pending preservation in Darlington works yard in August 1965. These were the last of T.W. Worsdell's most famous class. Both engines languished here until closure of the works in February 1966. No. 65099 failed to make it into preservation and was cut up on the spot as it was unfit to be moved. No. 65033 was transported to Beamish Open Air Museum where it was cosmetically restored. No. 65033 was an NER Class C no. 876, built at Gateshead works in 1889 and withdrawn from service in April 1962, surviving another two years after its epic exploits over Stainmore and Shap. Ironically, it had been withdrawn for scrap in 1939 but was reprieved owing to the outbreak of the Second World War. On 7 May 1960 it was the last Class J21 to cross the Stainmore line, the haunt of the class for half a century, and was the last engine to use Tebay turntable when it headed an RCTS/SLS special. It proceeded with three coaches over Shap summit unassisted taking 13½ minutes to do so – a fair performance for a seventy-year-old goods engine! The NER began building the Class C at Gateshead works in 1886 and 171 of the 201 total were built there. Darlington's contribution of 30 engines began in 1890 when 14 were built, with the other 16 being delivered the following year. (*Doug Hardy*)

Opposite above: Class J21 no. 65033 with the enthusiasts special at Barnard Castle on 7 May 1960 on its outward journey over Stainmore and Shap summits to Carlisle, returning to Darlington via Penrith and West Auckland. It had to stop for 20 minutes just before Stainmore summit for a blow up, although it later went unassisted over Shap. The author was aboard.

Opposite below: Class J27 no. 65819 ex-works waits on the dead line after a period of running-in. After a final trip to works for fine tuning it returned to one of the Blyth sheds in July 1963. It was withdrawn from there in October 1966.

Class V2 no. 60864 ex-works heads north with a tanker train through Glebe Road bridge at the end of December 1961. The final Class V2, no. 60836, was taken out of service from Dundee Tay Bridge shed at the end of December 1966. The last of Gresley's V2s, as well as his famous Pacifics, ended their days at Scottish sheds. No. 60864 was scrapped at North Road works in April 1964.

Class V2 no. 60885 with whitened buffers and smokebox fitting departs from platform no. 4 at Bank Top station, 6 October 1964. No. 60885 ended its days at Darlington, being withdrawn with classmate no. 60884 in August 1965. The driver can be seen, oil rag in hand, giving the guard a wave of acknowlegement before pulling away.

Class V2 no. 60901 heads north at Smithfield Road between the old south signal-box and an engineer's train in July 1964.

Class V2 no. 60808 with special train 1X78 on 21 July 1964, heading south on the Up main to Catterick Camp, where the engine would run round the train and return chimney first. A Darlington engine, it was withdrawn in October 1964.

Class J39/1 no. 64851 from Tyne Dock shed, a Gresley freight design of 1926, has been called in for scrap. Although approximately twenty years older, Wilson Worsdell's Class P3s (J27) were preferred for coal traffic and outlived the J39s, as did Raven's Class Q6 0–8–0s of 1913 vintage.

Class K1 no. 62008 awaits its next turn at Bank Top shed on 29 June 1965. The front end embellishments were a feature of the last three or four years of operation. The shed yard is beginning to look a bit untidy. Today, the whole shed site is a scene of total desolation, being used as a fly-tipping area for builders' rubble and domestic rubbish. Birch trees, weeds and bushes have claimed any free areas. No buildings remain and the only clue as to what had been there before is the 5yd wide strip of concrete that once spanned the full width of the front of the shed and in which the lines can still be counted, set into the concrete.

Class B16/2 no. 61475 on the works line at Bank Top shed on its way to the scrapyard from Hull Dairycoates shed in June 1963. No. 61475 was a Gresley rebuild in 1937 of Raven's original design of 1920.

Class B16/3 4–6–0 no. 61449 also heading for Darlington scrapyard in July 1963. This is Thompson's 1944 attempt to improve the design. The final batch went for scrap in July 1964.

Ex-LMS 2–6–4T no. 42639 at Bank Top shed on 4 May 1963. It arrived at Darlington in December 1961 with a motley collection of other LMS tanks, nos 40190, 42085, 42477 and 42553. No. 42639, a Stanier tapered-boiler design of 1935, left Darlington for Wakefield shed in June 1964, but lasted only until the following October when it was withdrawn from service.

The south end of
Darlington shed,
c. 1960. The engines
in view are (from
left to right) a
named Class B1,
Class A5/2 no.
69841, Ivatt Class
2MT no. 46477,
Class A3 no. 60038
Firdaussi, Class
A5/2 no. 69834 and
Class L1 no. 67729.
The shed was
reconstructed into
its final form in
1938.

Class J27 no. 65790 passing behind
North Road station en route to
Shildon or Faverdale wagon works
with a train of cut timber in March
1950. The engine looks ready for a
visit to North Road works. (*Geoff
Jackson*)

A view of the works line, known
locally as the 'dead line'. This consisted
of two parallel lines approximately 300
yds long on the north-east side of Bank
Top shed where locomotives were left
to cool off and were emptied of coal
before being towed across town to the
works or scrapyard.

Class A4 no. 60029 *Woodcock* speeding southwards at Snipe House junction, where Geneva curve bears round to the east. Opened in July 1887 the junction saw only occasional traffic. Northbound trains for Teesside would diverge at Northallerton. The triangle of land formed by the East Coast Main Line, the Saltburn branch and the Geneva curve was occupied by the Civil Engineers Reclamation Depot, which was served by Class Y1/1 vertical-boilered Sentinel locomotive no. 68153 (Departmental no. 54).

Class K1 no. 62059 trundles south with a train of flat wagons on 3 May 1963. Its last major repair was at Cowlairs works in Glasgow in 1966 when it was out-shopped on 22 September. It also proved to be Cowlairs' last major steam overhaul before the works closed. The North British Locomotive Co., also a Glasgow firm, built the K1s and it seems fitting that Cowlairs works should carry out its final repair on an engine built in the city.

Class K1 no. 62048 on the Up slow line with a dozen sheeted wagons and a guard's van in July 1962. The passenger coach on the left was shuffled around Bank Top station for some considerable time, but its purpose wasn't clear. Darlington had an allocation of eleven K1s in mid-1962, no. 62048 included. It finished up at a Chesterfield scrapyard in January 1968.

Class K1 no. 62044 heads north with a mixed freight on 6 July 1963, while Ivatt Class 4MT no. 43057 passes under Glebe Road bridge in the distance. Although modern and very successful, the K1s unfortunately had a life of only fifteen years or so because of the elimination of steam. Thompson developed the prototype K1s from Gresley's Class K4s in 1945; these Peppercorn modified further and production of the finalised version began in 1949. In all, 70 were built by the North British Locomotive Co. and although it was an LNER design they were delivered to the newly nationalised British Railways, which numbered them 62001–70. The prototype no. 61997 was classified K1/1.

Class K1 no. 62001 heads south past Bradbury signal-box in July 1964 with a load of steel sections. It had been to North Road works for a general overhaul in January of that year.

Class J25 no. 65713 at Bank Top shed on 5 August 1960 on its way to the scrapyard from one of the Blyth sheds. A visually pleasing design, the J25s were very similar to the J21 class in appearance, although they were not designed by the same engineer. The J21s appeared in 1886 to Thomas William Worsdell's design, while the J25s appeared in 1898 to his brother Wilson Worsdell's design and were slightly heavier and more powerful. The J25's boiler was compatible with the J21 and several other NER classes. Forty J25s were built at Darlington in 1898–9 as NER Class P1s, and another eighty were built at Gateshead.

Class J25 no. 65670 at Darlington scrapyard, 11 January 1962. Designed by Wilson Worsdell in 1898 the last of them were scrapped in 1962. Sister engine no. 65695 was actually given a full general overhaul at North Road works as recently as May 1960. No. 65670 was built at Gateshead works in 1899 as NER no. 2000 and classified P1. It was originally withdrawn from service in May 1939 from Tyne Dock shed, but was reinstated to working stock in November the same year after the outbreak of the Second World War, when it was sent to work on the Great Western Railway until the war finished in 1945. It was returned to Tyne Dock and renumbered NER no. 2050.

Class Q6 no. 63346 heads north on the Down main with a train of Esso tank wagons on 20 July 1963. The train is passing the site of Darlington's most serious railway accident. Twenty-five passengers were killed here on the night of 27 June 1928, when a Scarborough to Newcastle passenger train ploughed into another train which had been shunted into its path. Another accident only nine months later (9 March 1929) resulted in two more deaths.

Pioneer Standard Class 3MT no. 77000 comes off shed across Yarm Road bridge in May 1963. Only twenty were built; they had a very distinctive appearance with a high running plate fully exposing all the wheels and motion. With a tall chimney and taper boiler they looked like a GWR/Ivatt Class 2 hybrid, and proved to be very good engines. Built in 1954, no. 77000 was withdrawn from Stourton shed, Leeds, in November 1966.

Class A4 no. 60024 *Kingfisher* being reassembled in Darlington works on 8 August 1964. By then Doncaster had finished with steam repairs, its future being with modern traction. Darlington works had no future but was still busy with steam repairs including Doncaster's Pacifics.
(*Doug Hardy*)

Class K1 no. 62043 waits on the bridge spanning Yarm Road with St John's Church in the background, 6 July 1963. The crest on the bridge support depicts Darlington's coat of arms. No. 62043 was withdrawn from service while at Darlington shed in 1965, and was sold to T.W. Ward's scrapyard at South Bank, Middlesbrough. The buildings behind the billboards belong to the Grey Horse public house and the East End Working Men's Club.

Class K1 no. 62041 working hard with a freight approaching Salters Lane North on 23 April 1963. Note the allotments on top of the cutting – a common feature along railways anywhere in the country at this time. The Robert Stephenson's & Hawthorn locomotive works was situated off Thompson Street East to the left of the bridge in view. The company relocated to Darlington from Newcastle in 1901; bought by English Electric and stripped of its customer base, it closed in 1964. Springfield signal-box was located on the far side of Thompson Street East bridge on the Up side (to the left), but this became redundant in 1954 and its operations were taken over by Parkgate signal-box.

Class J39/2 no. 64917 waits outside the stripping shop on 29 June 1963. It was displaced from Tweedmouth shed as the Northumbrian branches closed. The bogie in the foreground seems to have run into some stiff opposition.

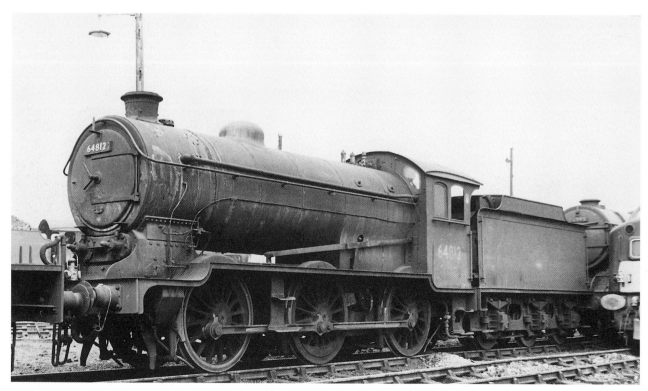

Class J39/1 no. 64812 at Darlington shed on 27 April 1963, having arrived from Blaydon shed for scrapping. Darlington was inundated with surplus J39s at this time. Class V2 no. 60949 is also awaiting the works.

Class J94 no. 68024 passing over Smithfield Road on the 27 July 1963 with a freight train for Croft yards. The driver looks very relaxed. A total of 75 J94s were bought from the Ministry of Supply in 1946. There were no variations in design, although a few from the Cromford & High Peak system carried the number on the bunker.

A Class V2 takes an interesting variety of parcel vans north towards Haughton Bridge, past the railcar depot, on 3 May 1963. The V2s were a very successful passenger or express freight engine developed from Gresley's Class A3 Pacifics. A class of large 3-cylinder engines, North Road produced 159 of the total number 184. Classes V2, B1, 8F and A2 were the mainstays of new engine production at the works during and immediately after the war years.

A wave from the driver as Class V2 no. 60954 takes a mixed freight north through Green Lane bridge in April 1963. This engine was called into works in November 1963 and scrapped. It was already on borrowed time as it had had an accident at Mirfield in March 1962, after which it spent a few days in the scrapyard before the works reprieved it and repaired it for another eighteen months of service.

Class B1 no. 61337 heading south towards Darlington passes the quarry at Aycliffe village with a mixed freight on 5 April 1963. Aycliffe parish church, St Andrew's, is on the skyline. The embankments are now overgrown with large bushes and trees, and so you couldn't take a picture from this location today. This engine, along with nos 61030 and 61306, were the very last B1s, being withdrawn from Low Moor shed, Bradford, in September 1967. Nos 61306 and 61264 survive in preservation. The last two to be actually cut up were nos 61050 and 61315 (Departmental nos 30 and 32 respectively) in April 1968 at Derby works. Darlington works built 60 and scrapped 48 of the 410 total built.

Postscript

D arlington's railway legacy has been badly neglected over the years. The Great North of England locomotive shed at Albert Hill is semi-derelict and hidden in a jungle of bushes and rubbish. The S&D carriage works at Hopetown is very shabby externally and the NER engine shed at Whessoe crossing still stands in industrial use amid scrap and second-hand cars. The Skerne Bridge is in a derelict industrial setting, while the disused S&D trackbed is no more than an overgrown narrow footpath. Darlington Railway Preservation Society's yard contains hopelessly delapidated rolling stock and both outer ends of the museum are neglected.

Several other towns with only a fraction of Darlington's railway history have developed and integrated their assets to include a working steam railway. Land is available for development at North Road Museum and there are 35 miles of virtually disused track to Weardale and access to the national network a few yards away. It's probably too late now for a steam centre, but surely what does remain could be made visitable? On a more positive note, the museum itself, the A1 'Tornado' project and the Darlington Railway Preservation Society's workshops are well worth a visit. The North East Locomotive Preservation Group (NELPG) is now moving into one end of the S&D carriage works. My feeling is that Darlington, despite its great historical railway importance, has failed to take advantage of that legacy and missed a great opportunity to build on the worldwide fame it already has as the birthplace of the railways.

One of the last jobs for Darlington works was to straighten out Britannia no. 70004 *William Shakespeare*, seen here outside the stripping shop on 18 December 1965. According to the painted-on shed code (9B) this engine was from Stockport shed. (*Doug Hardy*)

Index